The Secret
of a
Winning Culture

The Secret of a Winning Culture

Building High-Performance Teams

Larry E. Senn

John R. Childress

Foreword by Warren Bennis

Library of Congress Catalog Card Number: 99-067643

Larry E. Senn

The Secret of a Winning Culture: Building High-Performance Teams

Includes index.

1. Corporate Culture. 2. Culture Change. 3. Reengineering.
4. Change Initiatives. 5. Change Management. 6. High-Performance Culture. I.
Senn, Larry E. II. Childress, John R. III. Title.
IV. Title: The Secret of a Winning Culture: Building High-Performance Teams

ISBN 0-9648466-3-2 (paperback)

First printing, August 2002

Printed in Canada

printing number
1 2 3 4 5 6 7 8 9 0

Copies of *The Secret of a Winning Culture: Building High-Performance Teams* are available at special discounts for bulk purchases by corporations, institutions, and other organizations.

Please see the back of the book for an order form, or, for more information, please call:

ACKNOWLEDGMENTS

Like the team-based firm we run, this book has been the work of many people. In more ways than can be described, the team of consultants and staff of the Senn-Delaney Leadership Consulting Group has supported our writing, challenged and built upon our ideas, given us examples from their consulting engagements, read through countless drafts, and offered significant suggestions. Bernadette Senn and Scott Tempel helped rewrite a few of the chapters when we had significant "lapses" and the words just wouldn't come. Many consultants offered useful input, including: Joe Doyle, Paul Walker, Ernie Webb, John Clayton, Bob Carroll, and graphics designer, Peter Brown.

Our clients (all of whom we count as friends) have opened their organizations to our probing and offered examples of "the good, the bad, and the spectacular" from their experiences with culture change and leadership issues. Most notable among these have been John P. DesBarres and Nick Neuhausel of Transco Energy Company; Ron Burns, formerly of Enron; John Croom and the executives at the Columbia Gas System; and Ray Smith, John Gamba and Brenda Morris at Bell Atlantic Corporation.

We especially want to thank Dick Love who heads the manufacturing and reengineering efforts at Hewlett-Packard for reviewing our first draft and providing some valuable suggestions.

Many of our associations with other firms are opportunities for us to continue to grow, and none has been more developmental for us than our work with George and Linda Pransky of Pransky & Associates, located in LaConner, Washington. Their work on the Psychology of Mind is expressed in Chapters 8 and 11 as we explore "states of mind," "moods," and "assuming innocence in others." They help us to walk each day with grace and ease, regardless of what challenges are thrown our way.

We thank our partners, Yvonne Vick, Jim Ondrus, Rena Jordan, Mike Marino, and Paul Nakai for picking up some of the extra load while we spent time on this project. And a special thanks to Judy Gesicki for helping with and overseeing the transcription and typing.

Finally, to our children, Melia Childress, and Kevin, Darin, Jason, and Kendra Senn, for being the best teachers we have had on leadership and human dynamics.

FOREWORD

Foreword
by
Warren Bennis

Never before in the history of business has the impact of organizational culture been more critical to the success of organizations and the effectiveness of individuals leading them. The pace of change is so rapid that agile cultures, driven by high-performance teams, have become a competitive imperative. The knowledge and skills required to lead 21st-century organizations have changed dramatically.

Today, most books and articles written on organizational change acknowledge the power of culture. We often see cultural issues at the heart of the clash of mergers: the failure of strategies or change initiatives. Unfortunately, culture is much like the weather—everyone talks about it with the assumption that nothing can be done about it. We thrive when the sun shines and take cover when the winter winds blow. Fortunately, organizational culture is not quite so capricious. We are capable of charting a course through rain, sleet, snow, and fair weather if we can maintain our sense of direction, understanding the values and behaviors that lie at the core of our organizations. *The Secret of a Winning Culture* provides an excellent guidance system for navigating these evolving cultural landscapes. The book's ideas, tools, and techniques can change any team you lead or any culture you are a part of, large or small, into one that is healthy and high-performing.

In today's complex workplace, a leader's success is directly related to the effectiveness of his teams. Those teams make up the culture of the organization, and their health is a reflection of that culture's health. To realize the high-performance results we are after, we have to understand the power of these essential and healthy collaborations.

In a book I co-authored titled *Co-Leaders,* David Heenan and I make the point that the genius of our age is truly collaborative. Because of the complexity of the issues we face, we need teams of leaders working toward a common purpose. We no longer live in a world in which individual stars can carry the day on their own. To truly succeed, we need high-performance teams and winning cultures. *The Secret of a Winning Culture* provides insight into the role corporate culture plays in all change initiatives. It offers practical ideas that can be successfully implemented and will allow you, your team, and your organization to produce better results while supplying the personal fulfillment necessary for cultures to prosper.

My colleagues and I at the University of Southern California have been immersed in the study of leadership for many years. During that same period the authors, Larry Senn and John Childress, and their teammates at Senn-Delaney Leadership have been working with and studying the impact of culture on organizational effectiveness. Long before the word Culture appeared in a business journal, Larry became intrigued with the personality of organizations. It was 30 years ago, as a doctoral student here at USC, that he completed the first systematic study of corporate culture and its impact on the results of organizations. Over the past 20 years, he and his organization have worked on the cultural aspects of mergers and acquisitions, on shifting cultures for deregulation, on privatization in Europe, and on the fast-paced Silicon Valley cultures. No one has had more experience in identifying the secret of a winning culture than the authors of this book.

Warren Bennis

Warren Bennis is the founding chairman of the Leadership Institute, University of Southern California, a distinguished professor of business administration at the University of Southern California, and a consultant to multinational companies and governments throughout the world.

TABLE OF CHAPTERS

·

INTRODUCTION: NEW TIMES CALL FOR WINNING TEAMS AND HIGH-PERFORMANCE CULTURES

We are in one of those great historical periods that occur every 200 to 300 years when people don't understand the world anymore, and the past is not sufficient to explain the future. We are in a period of time in which companies will have to innovate quickly and be global to succeed.

—Peter Drucker

Several years ago, we noted dramatic changes affecting our clients. Our curiosity led us to undertake an interesting research project. We interviewed more than 100 leaders and leadership experts, from Bill Gates to Jack Welch and Warren Bennis to John Kotter, and asked them the question, "How will we need to lead differently as we enter the 21st century?"

All agreed that the game rules had changed and that traditional 20th-century leaders and organizations had to make some fundamental shifts. Key among those was a need to shift the historic leadership style and the habits, or culture, of organizations.

The classic top-down, hierarchical, turf-based organization was just not flexible, agile, or fast enough for the 21st century. The book that resulted from that research—*21st Century Leadership: Dialogues with 100 Top Leaders,* by Lynne J. McFarland, Larry E. Senn, and John R. Childress—began to describe what this high-performance culture would look like through the eyes of the leaders we interviewed. Thomas Gerrity, dean of the Wharton School of Business, said in one of those interviews, "Whole new paradigms for leadership are required for this crucial time in history because the old paradigms don't fit anymore. Workplace and social environments are changing very rapidly and people are also changing. The ability to learn, to adapt, to look freshly at the situation and not be entrapped by old models, constructs, or paradigms, is crucial to going forward."

During the past few years, we have had additional insights about the times we are in and the prices that individuals and families are paying. One of these realizations is that this past decade of turmoil and the high rate of change will be with us for a long time. There are no "kinder and gentler times" just over the horizon or around the corner. We are going to have to learn to live with rapid change, for our organizations and ourselves.

We have found even the most successful high-tech teams focusing more on teamwork. When we asked the head of a "most admired company" why he thought that was important, he said, "With the rapid pace of change and the shortened product cycle times, we can't afford any loose linkage."

Another common theme we have heard is, "I don't think I can work any harder or faster. I can already smell the clutch burning." One of the old habits many people are carrying forward from the past is a belief that our work ethic alone will get us through. We don't believe the answer lies in more and more hours and "nose to the grindstone" behaviors. The competitive game we are playing is a long-term, not a short-term, game, and people are already feeling excessive, unhealthy stress and a lack of balance in their lives. The answer to today's business and personal challenges does not lie in harder or more frantic effort. We believe it lies in creating an organization in which things happen with greater ease—one with more collaboration instead of turf—and wiser, more thoughtful decisions. It lies in personally working like an athlete in the "zone," in ease and grace, while achieving superior results.

We are convinced the answer lies in creating healthier, more balanced high-performance cultures where individuals can find balance and fulfillment in their professional and personal lives. It lies in developing the leadership skills that allow people to achieve more success with less stress.

The Secret of a Winning Culture: Building High-Performance Teams is designed to provide a blueprint to construct that winning culture in an organization or a team. In today's highly complex environments, a business culture is made up of a collection of teams. The secret is to develop the values and behaviors necessary to create high-performance teams, which through their interactions with each other, create high-performance cultures and winning organizations.

The ideas for this book have come from what we have learned in 20 years of consulting with hundreds of organizations and over 200,000 managers. Our purpose is to convey a series of principles and processes for building winning cultures and winning teams. These principles best ensure the success of change initiatives and help organizations, teams, and individuals accomplish their objectives.

Over the past two decades, we have committed ourselves to learning all we could about corporate culture, vision, and values, change management, leadership development, team-building, and performance improvement. In doing so, we have been personally moved and changed by the very nature of the work we do. To work with individuals who are struggling with difficult business (and sometimes personal) issues; to listen to their "visions" and their hopes and fears, and to hear their concerns for their employees, their beliefs in their products, and their desire to satisfy their customers, has been humbling, and at the same time, exhilarating. Nowhere can one be simultaneously more humbled and uplifted than during the processes of shifting corporate cultures and building winning teams.

Our sincere desire is that this book and the ideas and examples contained in it will be of value to you as you work at improving the lives of your employees, the effectiveness of internal teams, and the spirit and performance of your organizations. With these ideas put into practice, we have the best shot ever at creating the ultimate win-win-win situation—for all employees, customers, and shareholders!

John R. Childress and Larry E. Senn

1

THE JAWS OF CULTURE

WHY CHANGE INITIATIVES FAIL: IT'S THE CULTURE, DUMMY!

Between plans and reality lie years of habits, customs, unwritten ground rules, parochialism, and vested interests: the corporate culture. Culture cannot only stop a change effort dead in its tracks, it can also propel it to great heights. Wisdom is understanding the power of culture and how to get it to work for you, instead of against you, during organizational change.

Why is it that initiatives and strategies with great promise don't live up to their expectations? A window of competitive opportunity is evident; sound planning and processes are often in place, but the advantage doesn't fully materialize.

The story often sounds like some version of the following:

The numbers showed the merger would really pay off, but we've lost some key customers: Our best executives are leaving for other companies, and we seem to be having a real clash of cultures.

The reorganization was supposed to have broken down the barriers between divisions and created a more collaborative organization. Instead, we seem to have created new boundaries and turf issues.

The new strategy sounded great, but we haven't been able to execute it with our slow-moving, risk-averse bureaucratic culture.

The new I.T. system was supposed to be up and running last quarter, saving us time and money. There is a lot of finger-pointing going on now because it's behind schedule and it looks like it won't deliver all we thought it would.

*The analysis showed we'd make dramatic savings through reengi-
neering, but they haven't come through yet. Where are the results?
And why is everyone so upset?*

*We just completed another record quarter, and I know I should be feel-
ing good. The fact is, I'm paying too big a price personally to get
results around here and I don't know if I want to stay in this game.*

*We've got a few great quality improvement teams in place, but it is not
widespread. We haven't been able to build it into the fabric of the organization.*

More than just anecdotal evidence exists that change initiatives
fail more often than they succeed.

A *Harvard Business Review* article by Nohia and Berkley cites a
survey showing that 75 percent of the managers polled were
unhappy with change initiatives underway. Since the current business environment warrants these initiatives, why do they fail?

The answer is clear. Most change initiatives focus on the oper-
ational and technical side. What they too often ignore, or, at best,
give lip service to, is the human side—the behavioral side of
change. Anyone who has ever attempted to implement a change of
any kind has experienced the phenomenon of resistance to change
by people and institutions.

Such was our experience in our early history as performance
improvement consultants. We found that:

**It was easier to decide on change than to get people to
change!**

People and organizations are creatures of habit, and changing
habits is much harder than changing structures or systems. It
seemed to us that organizations, like people, had personalities,
and to ignore or not deal with an organization's personality traits
could be fatal to our change efforts. At that time, few knew what
we were talking about, and we were the only "culture shaping"
game in town.

Today, people recognize those personality traits as **Corporate
Culture**, and the business world is slowly beginning to appreciate

the power of cultural habits. Most change initiatives have at least token elements of "change management." Unfortunately, most organizations don't address cultural barriers as vigorously or systematically as needed.

We have long known that the only way to ensure the maximum success of any broad-based change initiative is to systematically deal with the corporate culture.

To truly change the corporation, you need to change the culture.

It is also interesting to note that James Champy, in *Reengineering Management*, states:

> *Everything we've learned drives toward one solid conclusion: The rules of governance (and self-governance) for effective business enterprises today are being determined by their culture, not their organizational structure.*

In the past two decades, many new approaches have emerged to improve business performance. Too often, however, a new theory appears and is hailed as "the answer" only to be later tossed aside as ineffective. We now know that this repeating pattern has less to do with the quality of the ideas than it does with the corporate culture that ground it down.

Trying to apply improvement methods to an unreceptive culture is like trying to apply a Band-Aid underwater. There's nothing wrong with the Band-Aid, but it won't stick and therefore it's ineffective. Some organizations benefited greatly from self-managed teams, empowerment, or TQM, but most tried them, decided they didn't work, and moved on to the next quick fix. It wasn't that the theories didn't have value (even when they weren't absolutely perfect), it's that they were applied to an incompatible culture where the new approaches couldn't "take."

The reason it's hard to implement change, that teams are often dysfunctional, and people are so stressed at work, is because of what we call the Jaws of Culture.

The Jaws of Culture

A corporation's culture can be its greatest strength when it is consistent with its strategies. But a culture that prevents a company from meeting competitive threats, or from adapting to changing economic or social environments, can lead to the company's stagnation and ultimate demise.

—Business Week

More change initiatives, from strategy to I.T. systems to merger to reengineering, fail as a result of cultural issues than any other single factor. If the cultural barriers were well understood and addressed, a much higher percentage of change efforts would achieve their potential.

Just a few of the cultural barriers that cause change initiatives to fail are

- Hierarchical structure and top-down leadership style
- Internal competition between departments—turf and "we-they"
- Heavy entitlement mind-set and poor empowerment
- Lack of accountability, excessive blaming
- An "observer-critic" culture that kills new ideas
- Communication barriers
- Resistance to changing the status quo
- Reinforcement systems that ignore customer satisfaction
- Non-participative management style—boss-driven command and control
- Lack of trust in the company and between groups
- Top management calls for behavior change but doesn't walk the talk

All change initiatives must pass through the Jaws of Cul ture — most get chewed-up, spit out, and forgotten long before they ever accomplish their objectives. The jaws consist of the major cultural barriers that form the ingrained habit patterns of company and individual behavior.

While each company and each team is different, they all have their own barriers that comprise their "Jaws of Culture." What are yours?

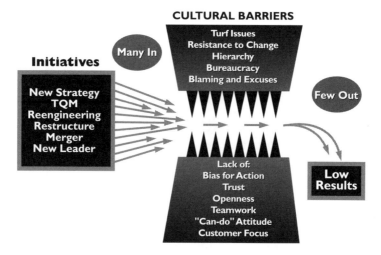

© 1999 Senn Delaney Leadership Consulting Group, Inc.

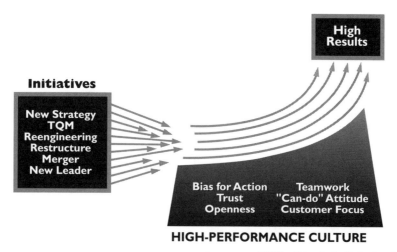

© 1999 Senn Delaney Leadership Consulting Group, Inc.

Figure 1

Mergers and Cultural Clash

Increased competition, deregulation, privatization, and the global-ization of markets have created special needs, including:

- A requirement for greater size or scale to better compete
- A need for broader competitive skills through alliances and acquisitions
- A need to create broader geographic presence or coverage

Mergers and acquisitions are becoming a key part of many orga-nizational strategies during these turbulent times. For some com-panies, it is the only way to significantly grow in order to compete with the bigger players in their industry. While it is clear that a merger or acquisition must be based on solid financials and other objective elements like strategic fit, ignoring the corporate culture can be a recipe for disaster. Far too often, differences in manage-ment styles and cultures are not considered during the pre-acqui-sition evaluation process. As a result, many acquisitions that looked very promising from a strategic or financial viewpoint in the pre-merger phase fall apart in the implementation phase.

Examples of the impact of culture on the success of mergers and acquisitions can be found regularly in business journals and news-papers:

When the deal is inked and the financial wizards go home, that's when the trouble starts. You've got the numbers. Now, what are you going to do about the people?

Training Magazine, "The Forgotten Factor in Mergers"

When companies combine, a clash of cultures can turn potentially good business alliances into financial disasters.

Psychology Today, "The Merger Syndrome"

Only half of the mergers end up on a happy note.

Author Unknown

A mismatch of cultures was a key factor that led to the failed acquisition of NCR by AT&T. By the end of 1995, AT&T's losses had reached two billion dollars. While the two companies looked similar on the surface, their cultures were very different in significant ways. NCR was highly conservative and AT&T was politically correct. NCR has always been tightly controlled from the top while AT&T was more decentralized. AT&T was unionized; NCR nonunion. They tried to share manufacturing facilities, but had to give up on it due to lack of compatibility. In an article in *The Economist*, the director of the British arm of AT&T said, "The president told everyone they were empowered. The problem was, that left some important decisions in the wrong hands!" *The Economist* article ends by saying, "The acquisition turned what might have been a crisis for NCR into a death watch."

Increasing evidence exists that cultural incompatibility is the largest cause of 1) poor merger performance, 2) departure of key executives, and 3) time-consuming conflicts when trying to integrate organizations. In a survey conducted by the Bureau of Business Research at American International College, the CFO and other key financial executives from 45 Fortune-500 firms (total sales over $240 billion), said that incompatibility of the corporate cultures, much more than financial or planning mistakes, is the most likely and damaging factor that prevents mergers and alliances from achieving their desired synergy.

Two companies merging based on financial data alone would be like two people marrying based on height, weight, and vital statistics—both lead to high divorce rates. The answer lies in dealing more systematically with the cultural aspect of the merger.

CULTURE AND THE NEW LEADER

Have you ever wondered why a CEO or other leader who was very successful at one firm has a hard time getting on track when they move to a new firm? In more cases than not, they have not figured out the culture or been able to overcome it.

WESTINGHOUSE: NEW LEADER STRUGGLES

Wall Street applauded when Michael Jordan, a retired PepsiCo executive, took the helm at Westinghouse Electric Corp. and expected quick results. Jordan, however, is finding that change comes slowly at Westinghouse and admits that a turnaround will take a few years. Besides the business difficulties, he's also struggling with a culture clash. His cost-cutting, personal accountability approach tends to run counter to Westinghouse's more rigid style, in which managers rarely tend to outperform financial goals. One of Jordan's actions has been to unbundle the company and let go of the older, harder-to-change manufacturing culture.

JAWS AND REENGINEERING

Nowhere is the impact of culture more evident than in reengineering. With the best intentions, hundreds of companies have embarked on reengineering efforts only to run into brick walls. More often than not, their efforts were derailed and reengineering became another failed "flavor of the month" improvement process.

Unfortunately, reengineering disappointments are the rule rather than the exception.

According to Michael Hammer, his earlier prediction of a two-thirds failure rate still stands nearly two years after corporations jumped head-long into reengineering efforts. And the failure rate may be even higher.

A study conducted by Arthur D. Little, Inc. reported that only 16 percent of 350 executives interviewed said they were fully satisfied with the results of their reengineering efforts. In fact, 68 percent of these executives reported that their reengineering efforts created additional problems that were unintended at the beginning of the process (*Information Week*, June 20, 1994).

REENGINEERING REPORT CARD

North America and Europe (99 companies)

16%	**Extraordinary Results**	A
17%	**Strong Results**	B
42%	**Mediocre to Marginal**	C/D
25%	**Failed—No Results**	F

Adapted from: State of Reengineering Report: CSC Index, 1994

There are many reasons for failure. In an article titled, "No Need for Excuses," Michael Hammer and Steven Stanton suggest that there are, fundamentally, two causes for reengineering failure: Failures of Intellect (information and understanding) and Failures in Leadership! They conclude the reason for the large number of reengineering failures lies not in the process of reengineering itself, but in the leadership and in human dynamics.

Not only have the results often suffered in reengineering, but the human price has been enormous. The typically mechanical "engineering" approach to change has neglected the heart of organizations—the people and the culture. It is no wonder that reengineering has become a negative word in the business world and is rapidly losing favor with companies and consultants.

You Can't Get There From Here

For anyone who has been through a performance improvement effort, it doesn't take studies to prove that cultural or "people" issues are often significant barriers to success.

Unfortunately, corporate leaders all too often underestimate the difficulty of implementing a dramatic shift in performance.

The shift from the old ways of doing things to new, untested ways is wrenching and leaves every person involved in a state of uncertainty and confusion. Will the new ways work? What will my role be? Will I be able to handle the new work? Will I have a new boss who will treat me fairly? Will I like my new co-workers? Will I still have my place in the new scheme of things?

Jack Welch of GE summarizes his thoughts on the difficulty of implementing a major change initiative and what is required for success:

> *When I try to summarize what I've learned, one of the big lessons is that change has no constituency. People like the status quo. They like the way it was. When you start changing things, the good old days look better and better.*

THE SHORTFALL IN TQM

In our work to help clients revitalize or kick-start TQM efforts, we typically encounter the following scenario—the story is a familiar one. The leaders have openly declared their commitment to become a total quality organization, usually with all-employee rallies, internal news articles, and lots of fanfare. Functions have been set up to manage the process. The company has invested fairly heavily in educating most people in the tools of quality. They have established quality improvement teams and set up awards and recognition programs to acknowledge gains.

Unfortunately, they find that while a few quality teams do well, the quality process does not become a way of life in the organization. In most cases, we find the culprit is the corporate culture. Few employees really speak up with improvement ideas because the culture is hierarchical and boss-driven: resistance to change is high, and ideas are too narrow to be implemented because the organization is turf-based, not boundary-less.

It is true that TQM programs have been of benefit to many organizations, but all too often they have not reached their potential. A 1994 Roth and Strong Survey of 186 senior executives from numerous leading U.S. manufacturing and service companies found only 41% satisfaction with the success of their TQM efforts. Like reengineering, the roots of TQM are also very mechanical and technical, having started as statistical quality control. The cultural and human aspects of the changes are underestimated and this creates the shortfall.

Strategy Implementation and Culture

Fewer firms today are diversifying far beyond their core businesses. This was not always the case. As the regional Bells and AT&T looked at coming deregulation, they saw an obvious need to diversify. An early example was NYNEX, which some years ago put billions into diversification, including computer stores and software companies. The strategies didn't succeed, and the reason is obvious. No two cultures could be more opposite than that of a historically regional monopoly and that needed by a retail store or software development firm. Retailers make major purchasing decisions based on 24-hour flash sales reports. They move fast, keep ahead of trends, and are sales and marketing-driven. Software development cultures are also characterized by speed and fast time-to-market. Telecommunications organizations are large and slow, capital-intensive, stable, reliable, high-cost, and operations-driven. This was a classic case of the culture not supporting the strategy. Today, NYNEX has taken its great culture and skills and built successful billion-dollar telephone businesses in Thailand and the U.K., using strategies that match their culture and their competencies. Their latest strategy is to gain scale through a merger with Bell Atlantic. The ultimate success of that strategy will largely be determined by how well they avoid culture clash.

The Cost of Culture

Culture barriers are often hidden in the fabric of the organization and are difficult to see without the aid of a comprehensive Culture Audit. Cultural barriers can quickly show up in dysfunctional behaviors once the change initiative begins. Key among the early behavioral signs of cultural resistance are

- Reluctance to accept ideas from other organizations (the "not invented here" syndrome)

- Turf issues and power struggles
- Groups forming under the protection of a politically strong individual that distance themselves from the change process
- Senior management having other priorities that prevent sufficient personal involvement and visibility
- Lip service and "malicious obedience"
- The "observer-critic" syndrome in which all new ideas are challenged
- People and groups blaming one another
- Hierarchical rigid structure
- Bureaucracy and resistance to change

Most organizations and leaders, no matter how successful, face some dysfunction in their teams. Getting results and implementing change extracts too high a price. What is the cost of your group or company's cultural barriers?

Reader Activity

The Cost of Culture

A recent study of Fortune 1000 companies by Accountemps estimated that 20% of people's time in an organization is wasted on issues related to the corporate culture. Our own observations indicate that time lost on just one cultural barrier—Victim Games—wastes at least this much time alone! These victim games induce blaming others, justifying poor performance, and complaining about what's not working or why things should be different. These are key elements of the cost of culture.

Check off below any of the cultural barriers you recognize in your own organization:

- ❏ Turf issues
- ❏ Resistance to change
- ❏ Hierarchical
- ❏ Bureaucratic
- ❏ Blaming and excuses
- ❏ Lack of customer focus
- ❏ Lack of bias for action
- ❏ Lack of trust
- ❏ Lack of openness
- ❏ Lack of teamwork
- ❏ Lack of can-do attitude

How much is your current corporate culture costing you in terms of lost dollars? The following is a simple and interesting worksheet that can help you get an estimate of the impact of culture on performance.

1. Assemble your management team and ask them each to write down an estimate of the percent of the work day that is lost to such cultural issues as complaining about other people, talking about management or other departments' actions, blaming others, finding excuses or fault, or complaining about lack of direction. Ask them to write down a percentage (usually it is between 5-25%) representing the time that is wasted and lost. You can also do it yourself to get your own estimates.

2. Add up everyone's estimates and get an average. _____ Average % of time lost

3. Next, determine the total number of employees in your company (or group).

    _____ Number of employees

4. Multiply employees by percent of lost time. This gives you the equivalent employees you would save or could be available to help get the work done.

What would be added to the bottom line? How much easier would the organization be to manage and how much more time would be available to get things done if this behavior were to discontinue?

2

THE POWER OF A HEALTHY CULTURE

CULTURE AS A LAUNCHING PAD

High-performance cultures are a launching pad for new initiatives. Winning behaviors, like a can-do spirit, bias for action, collaboration, mutual support, passion for the customer, openness to change, innovation, and positive attitudes, support the success of any initiative.

GE is widely recognized as one of the world's most successful business organizations. It consistently turns in record performance. What underlies GE's success is its focus on a core set of values called GE's Leaders' Values which define the culture. It really is the power of a healthy culture.

HEWLETT PACKARD

The importance of a healthy culture was dramatically illustrated by Forbes' selection of Hewlett Packard as America's best-performing company in their January 1996 issue. Hewlett Packard's profits were up 51 percent and their share price was up 90 percent. Unlike many companies, their improved profit had not come from massive layoffs and painful restructuring, but through growth—they are one of the only firms of their size that can sustain 20 percent-plus growth.

Culture has been important at Hewlett Packard since David Packard and Bill Hewlett established the values called "The HP Way." Packard, at 84, summed up his management philosophy as, "Get the right people, stress the importance of teamwork, and fire them up with the will to win." Hewlett and Packard created a culture unlike the hierarchical, bureaucratic, military model that is the heritage of large organizations. Historically, they have been far more egalitarian, innovative, and individualistic, and had a team-based structure years before teamwork was as valued in American business.

Lew Platt, the current HP CEO, says, "I spend a lot of my time talking about values rather than trying to figure out the business strategies. I don't think I realized until I became CEO (in 1992) how different that is."

His belief in the power of a healthy culture was summed up when he said, "The most important aspect of the management of this company is cultural control. Get that right and the rest follows."

It's interesting to note that HP has reached much the same conclusion that Peters and Waterman did in their 1982 landmark book, *In Search of Excellence.* They had used McKinsey and Co.'s 7S model to evaluate excellent companies. That model contained three objective, or "hard," Ss, and four subjective, or "soft," ones.

McKinsey 7 Ss

3 Objective or Hard Ss
- Strategy – plans and strategies
- Structure – organizational chart
- Systems – procedures

4 Subjective or Soft Ss
- Staff – type of personnel
- Style – style of management
- Skills – both interpersonal and technical
- Shared Values – culture

They found that while successful companies worked on all seven, they seemed to have much more appreciation and respect for the soft Ss. Of all of these, the most powerful one was the Shared Values, also called the Superordinate Goals that capture the vision and culture of the organization—like the HP Way.

THE 7-S FRAMEWORK

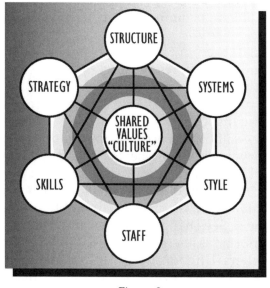

Figure 2

Source: McKinsey & Co. © 1999 Senn Delaney Leadership Consulting Company, Inc.

In a related book, *The Art of Japanese Management*, Tony Athos and Richard Pascale (also from McKinsey) explored in more depth the Seven Ss model. One of their conclusions was that the soft Ss, including Shared Values or Culture, are the least-publicized secret weapon of high-performing American firms. They go on to say that people "all too often observe them through traditional American cultural and managerial filters, and tend to assume that the 'soft S' factors are just froth. That 'froth' has the power of the Pacific."

Jack Welch, CEO of General Electric, came to similar conclusions in transforming GE. Most of his initial efforts were focused on the harder Ss, particularly Strategy and Structure. In time he found this wasn't enough. He concluded he also had to systematically transform the historic habits or culture of the organization. This led to his well-known "work out" sessions at Crotenville and the creation of GE's Leaders' Values.

GE LEADERS THROUGHOUT THE COMPANY HOLD THESE VALUES:

- Create a clear, simple, reality-based, customer-focused vision and be able to communicate it straightforwardly to all constituencies.
- Understand accountability and commitment and be decisive — set and meet aggressive targets — always with unyielding integrity.
- Have a passion for excellence — hate bureaucracy and all the nonsense that comes with it.
- Have the self-confidence to empower others and behave in a boundary-less fashion — believe in and be committed to Work.
- Have, or have the capacity to develop, global brains and global sensitivity and be comfortable building diverse global teams.
- Stimulate and relish change...do not be frightened or paralyzed by it. See change as opportunity, not just a threat.
- Have enormous energy and the ability to energize and invigorate others. Understand speed as a competitive advantage and see the total organizational benefits that can be derived from a focus on speed.

These values defined the new culture at GE and played a vital role in its transformation into a company that is a model of success.

NEW LEADERS AND CULTURAL CHANGE

New leaders have a window of opportunity to define both new team behaviors and shifts in cultural traits. David Novak was one such leader who did that well at KFC.

KFC

David is a dynamic leader who aggressively moved to shape an old American institution, Kentucky Fried Chicken. KFC had gone through a number of changes in ownership from The Colonel to John Y. Brown and, ultimately, to PepsiCo. David saw his job as leading the rebirth of a great American icon. His vision included shaping a new culture, refocusing on the customer, and rebuilding healthier relations with the large franchise organization. That process began with an off-site Leadership, Team-building, and Culture-Shaping retreat with the top-15 officers at KFC. The group agreed to focus all of the organization's attention on supporting the restaurants and restaurant general managers (RGMs) in order to better serve the customers. The theme they developed was "The RGM is No. 1—The Customer is the Reason Why." In a historic move, all 2,500 restaurant general managers were brought to Louisville to attend a seminar similar to the one the attended by the senior team. That session was used to support new products, gain commitment, implement new restaurant strategies, and increase commitment to higher levels of customer service. Several months after all those activities and the related reinforcement, KFC was leading the fast-food industry in terms of percent gained in sales. David is now repeating the process with Tricon, the restaurant group including KFC, Pizza Hut, and Taco Bell that was just spun off from PepsiCo.

BELL ATLANTIC

Ray Smith took over as CEO of Bell Atlantic not long after divestiture. The company had a successful history as a regional phone company and was made up of independent state phone companies. Smith himself had enjoyed independence as president of Bell of Pennsylvania, which he ran in a fairly autonomous way. While there was no strong hint that rapid deregulation would come to pass, he sensed he had to change both the strategy and the culture to be a winner in the future market. As Ray Smith once said, "There's a train coming down the track headed straight for us. You can't see it, but if you put your ear on the rail and listen closely, it's on its way. We are going to have to have a sense of urgency about teaching this elephant to dance (changing the culture) if we're going to move from being a regional monopoly to becoming a global competitor." Smith has moved aggressively on shifting the culture through a process called "The Bell Atlantic Way." It was been regarded as one of the faster-moving Bell companies.

SEARS

Arthur Martinez has had a dramatic impact on Sears as a new leader. His successful merchandising and sales-promotion focus on the "Softer Side of Sears" is well known. Less known is the work done to shift the culture including a major emphasis on a sales and customer service-oriented culture. Store managers and their teams in more than 500 stores have been through a series of leadership, team-building, and culture-shaping seminars. In a study of the most customer-oriented companies in America by The Knowledge Exchange, Sears was rated as the most improved service merchandising company in America.

*All three **new leaders** proved that their focus on culture did have a major impact on the results and the success of their organizations. They focused first on building an aligned team at the top and then on new behaviors in the organization through systematic culture-shaping initiatives.*

ADAPTING AN OLD CULTURE

Another example of the power of culture can be seen in IBM. When their culture matched the times and the strategy, they couldn't be stopped. Historically, they were at the vanguard of companies that adopted new improvement processes such as quality, empowerment, and customer service. When the times changed and the culture didn't, all these improvement efforts didn't stop IBM's downward momentum. By simply layering these processes onto an existing culture that was rigid, cautious, and fragmented, most of their power to effectively create change was lost. It has taken a revolution at the top of the organization, with the first-ever selection of an outsider as CEO, to begin to break the historic IBM culture and prepare the company for a new, faster-moving, more competitive marketplace. IBM is now making a comeback through a combination of strategies, including addressing culture change.

The culture of an organization must adapt to new business realities. What works at one stage in a company's growth may not work at a later stage. Very often, the culture that brought the organization success in its early years may be the very cause of a company's demise. The trick is to recognize this problem and look for ways to shift the culture. All too often, the temptation to work harder with old cultural behaviors can lead the organization down a path from which it is difficult to return.

Our own experience with clients undergoing significant process changes suggests that there are a number of cultural elements that must be in place for effective change to happen. The organization needs an understanding of the unwritten ground rules in the old culture. How the informal system has operated and how people are still connected to a process will also be needed to reshape the corporate culture, based on healthy shared values. This takes strong, inspiring, and committed leadership. One of the keys to making this happen is over-communication. Too much can't be said about the change in any and all directions. It is also important to be able to directly confront high-level backsliders in the process. To make this happen, however, requires a continuity of leadership: We don't want to change horses in midstream.

Perhaps the biggest factors in the culture that will instantly spell success or failure for change efforts are the degree of openness and trust and the ability of employees at all levels to engage in frank and honest discussions about the business. Without these as part of the corporate culture, implementation will be decidedly more difficult.

The real performance-enhancing value of change initiatives is gained only after fundamental changes in culture, organizational design, management style, leadership, and work practices have been undertaken by a company.

HARNESSING THE POWER OF A HEALTHY CORPORATE CULTURE

In this book, we lay out a blueprint for a culture change process that supports any performance-improvement initiative. The principles can be used by any leaders and their teams as well as by overall organizations. This is not a cosmetic make-over or a repackaging of motivation theories. Changing corporate culture requires a rethinking; a shift in our understanding of people and the people-side of organizational performance. It stretches and reformulates our paradigms of leadership.

Many people today are emphasizing the negatives in the

business environment—the loss of jobs, the lack of security, the loss of balance in life, and the high stress levels. This does not have to be the case. Today's business organizations have an incredible inherent level of potential. They have also come a tremendous way in improving many of the methods by which they have been operating over the past 20 years, an accomplishment that is not often noted. The power behind these changes and its future potential is the people in the organization and their collective values, beliefs, and norms — what is commonly called the corporate culture.

Once this source of power is energized and aligned with the organization's vision and goals, phenomenal improvements in performance and quality of life become almost routine. The following chapters will show you how to harness the incredible power of corporate culture and use it to supercharge all your performance improvement efforts.

3

ALIGNING STRATEGY, STRUCTURE, AND CULTURE

First we shape our institutions, and afterwards they shape us.

—Winston Churchill

As we have seen, the failure of many organizational improvement initiatives can generally be traced back to the corporate culture: people resisting change, poor leadership skills, people not knowing how to work together, or employees not understanding the new direction.

Before we can create a culture that supports change efforts, it's important to understand how a culture that works fine under one set of business circumstances can create failure in times of change. It helps to take a macro look at an organization as a working relationship between strategy, structure, and culture. The following model is one we have used extensively with clients to help them understand how change and culture interact and how corporate culture often acts as a barrier to strategic change.

Aligning Strategy, Structure, and Culture

Unless culture is properly aligned with business strategies, it is difficult, if not impossible, to implement a new strategic thrust to meet increased competition or changes in the marketplace. In fact, if the new strategies are dramatically different from the old, the culture is likely to conflict with the new direction. The new strategies will be ignored or sabotaged and will generally fail. An organization with a firmly embedded culture will find change slow, as the culture reinforces and perpetuates the status quo. Thus, the challenge of change is to shift the culture into alignment with the new business strategy.

In the early growth of an organization, a culture emerges that is influenced by and, in turn, is supportive of the organization's strategy and structure (Figure 3.1). One author insightfully describes culture as a group's shared learning as it struggles to survive in its environment; it is "the solution to external and internal problems that has worked consistently for a group..." (Edgar H. Schein, *How Culture Forms, Develops and Changes*). Thus, culture develops over time, evolving in response to the demands of the internal and external environment. While early cultures are relatively soft and formative, later they harden, taking on an existence of their own.

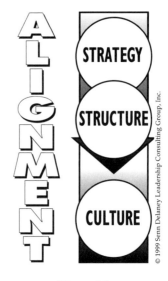

Figure 3.1

Within the U.S. retail industry, it is easy to see this model in action. Wal-Mart pursues a mass-merchandising discount strategy, while Nordstrom, also financially successful, depends on a strategy of providing a full line of soft goods with a significant focus on extraordinary customer service. Both Wal-Mart and Nordstrom are large, nation-wide organizations that have been able to evolve strong cultures that are in alignment with their respective strategies and structures.

Indeed, many industry observers agree that it is the strength of the Wal-Mart and Nordstrom cultures, which are very different yet equally strong, that make both organizations able to implement plans better than their competitors. While the competition may pursue similar strategies, they do so with less aligned or cohesive corporate cultures and achieve significantly less impressive results. Wal-Mart and Nordstrom developed completely different strategies, structures, and cultures, yet each organization is a highly aligned and productive organization with a vital competitive advantage.

When organizations face changes in their business environments, survival and prosperity often depend on their ability to quickly change directions. Generally this involves a shift in strategy followed by changes in organizational structure (Figure 3.2).

As new strategies are developed and new structures put into place, many employees continue to think and perform in ways that were developed within the old culture. These cultural habits and methods of working and managing are often at odds with the new strategy and organizational structure. While the corporate goals have shifted, the old ways of doing business are still in place and may now be in conflict with the new directions.

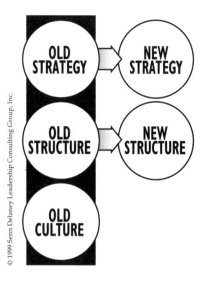

© 1999 Senn Delaney Leadership Consulting Group, Inc.

Figure 3.2

There are several signs that a corporate culture has gotten out of alignment with the organization's strategy and structure:

- Frequent reorganizations, but the same old problems persist
- Unwillingness to take risks, or make long-term commitments
- Resistance to new ways of doing things
- Lack of accountability — spending time blaming or finding fault
- Power plays and poor teamwork, causing costly project delay or errors
- Mistrust between management and employees
- Lack of clear vision or direction; people are confused about where they're going

In an organization that is out of alignment, more and more effort is required to make things work as the organization struggles to meet the challenges of today with the attitudes of yesterday. The result is often tension, resistance, and lowered morale instead of an effective, dynamic organization moving toward its goals (Figure 3.3).

The old culture anchors the organization in the past, preventing

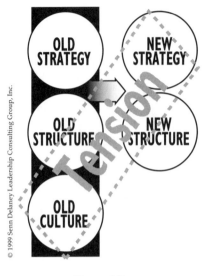

© 1999 Senn Delaney Leadership Consulting Group, Inc.

Figure 3.3

it from moving forward. This creates an increasing level of frustration that becomes especially pronounced when some employees have bought into the new way while others remain mired in the old. One manager described this stage of change as pushing a rope: "There's a great deal of effort expended, but it doesn't seem to get you anywhere."

The challenge of leadership is to shift the culture into alignment with the new strategy and structure. We like to think in terms of shifting a culture as opposed to replacing or changing it, as key cultural characteristics usually exist that should be retained and nurtured, while new characteristics will need to be added to make the culture more compatible with the new strategic thrust (Figure 3.4).

© 1999 Senn Delaney Leadership Consulting Group, Inc.

Figure 3.4

A "UNIVERSAL" EXAMPLE

The Bell Telephone System is a classic example of the effect of a changing industry on the alignment of strategy, structure, and culture. For more than half a century, "universal service, end-to-end" was the Bell corporate vision, and they were very good at it. Every component in the organization—financial policies, technology, pricing philosophy, product and market strategies, and organizational design—evolved to support this pervasive mission.

Overall, the Bell System's strategies were driven by regulatory and technological considerations. Financial policies were geared toward dividends, with a heavy debt structure and extensive external financing. Bell Laboratories, insulated in the regulated environment, was able to focus on basic research and technological opportunity without worrying about consumer preferences. Customer pricing, which was subsidized by the overall rate base, was based on the premise that everyone should be able to afford phone service. Marketing and product strategies focused on mass markets and standardized products. The corporate structure was large, centralized, and organized by function.

The Bell corporate culture included a regulatory mindset that favored adherence to policies and procedures, rigorous analysis of new projects and changes, and an elaborate approval process. The reward system fostered lifetime careers with a slow, steady progression and a strong focus on hierarchy. Other characteristics of the culture included dedication to customer service, group accountability, standardized procedures, and formal communication. The culture was ideally aligned with the organization's structure and strategy of universal service.

W. Brooke Tunstall, an AT&T vice president who was closely involved in the divestiture planning leading up to the 1984 breakup of AT&T, provides an inside view of the cultural dynamics at AT&T in his book *Disconnecting Parties*:

> *All these (cultural) attributes evolved to directly support one superordinate goal, universal service. In fact, everything related to the culture was affected by this goal; the kind of people we hired, their shared value systems, the infrastructure of processes*

to run the business. All were committed to the unchanging objective of providing high-quality service at affordable prices to everyone in the United States. Rarely, in fact, had corporate mission and corporate culture been so ideally matched.

In the years preceding the January 1984 divestiture, the telecommunications industry experienced a dramatic change as it began the shift from a monopolistic, regulated environment to a competitive, deregulated one. After divestiture, AT&T and the new "Baby Bells" responded with numerous changes in strategy and structure.

New strategic directions were driven by market opportunities and financial needs. Financial strategies were geared to meet earnings-per-share growth objectives, with a much lower debt structure. Research and design efforts would shift toward the application of technology to meet customer requirements. Markets would be segmented, with customized offerings. Finally, the organization would be restructured into smaller, more decentralized business units to better support the markets and the customer-driven strategies.

It's easy to imagine the tension as employees struggled to meet the demands of the new strategies with a culture that had previously been developed for the regulated business environment. Following the 1984 breakup, a corporate survey at AT&T asked 6,000 employees to share their thoughts and feelings surrounding various aspects of the divestiture and the new organ-izations. The findings revealed somewhat of an identity crisis for the AT&T employees:

I knew the old Bell system, its mission, its operation, its people, its culture. And I knew my niche in it. In that knowledge, I had identity and confidence about my company and myself. Now I work for a new company, one fourth its former size, with only a partial history and no track record. With the loss of our mission, Universal Service, and the fragmentation of the very business of providing telephone service, I find myself asking, "Who are we? Who am I?"

The 1984 divestiture created organizational chaos. Suddenly employees and organizations were in a world of competition where the ability to deliver the products and services customers preferred, at a price they were willing to pay, was critical to survival. While the leaders of these "new" organizations quickly recognized the need to change strategies and organizational structures, they soon found themselves with companies out of alignment. Over the past 10 years, the Baby Bells have struggled to shift their cultures. Some have been much more successful than others. And some have been re-merged with other Baby Bells as the industry has begun to come back together again. This, too, has presented unique problems as these newly founded cultures are now reforming into singular entities. Whether or not they can move fast and far enough to compete in the world of the Internet is still to be determined.

New Strategies and Old Cultures: A Design to Fail

In the business world prior to 1980, a relatively stable business environment supported cultures that were highly structured with carefully developed standards and procedures, clearly defined policies, multilayered organization charts, strong chain-of-command, deliberate approval processes, and a compensation system that rewarded playing by the rules. Since the game wasn't changing much, neither should the rules!

Today's current environment of increased global competition, rapid technological advances, worldwide economic fluctuations, and changing social norms and values has upset all the old rules and thrown out all the standard success formulas. These extraordinary changes are forcing today's business leaders to shift not only strategy and structure, but culture as well.

Jack Welch, chairman and CEO of GE, states that fundamental change is a fact of life that's here to stay:

> *Organizations are changing by necessity. Globalization is simply a fact of life. We have slower growth in the developed worlds. This puts more pressure on all of us since we are all after a piece of the pie. Therefore, value is all there is to provide. For example, in the computer business, if you miss a cycle you lose your company. So if you're going to provide the most value, if you're going to have the lowest cost and the highest quality product*

available, you've got to engage every mind that you hire. To have some minds idling in a stalled mode is unacceptable.

As companies scramble to change their strategy and structure, they're finding themselves anchored by a culture that's stuck in the old ways. Trying to implement new strategies and structures with an out-of-alignment culture creates a chaotic environment that spreads confusion, disrupts morale, and can actually lower productivity.

Even new high-tech companies face cultural challenges. Can they sustain the dramatic and hectic pace they had as start-ups? Will their fierce independence get in the way of team alignment as they create more products, more groups, and more acquisitions?

All companies, new and old, need to nurture and tend to their culture, much like a garden. It is the soil that all ideas and plans grow in. Fortunately, processes are available to ensure maximum crop yields through high-performance teams and cultures.

4

A MODEL FOR RESHAPING CORPORATE CULTURE

Necessity is the Mother of Invention

The culture change model presented in this book is the result of consulting work with large U.S., European, and multinational companies over the past 25 years and has proven to be effective in such diverse industries as financial services, health care, nuclear power, telecommunications, manufacturing, computers, aerospace, distribution, retailing, transportation, and gas and electric utilities.

There are no simple, magic formulas for organizational change; no quick fixes. However, there is a series of principles and processes for shifting culture that, when led by senior management, has proven to be highly effective. An overview of the model is described below. Each phase of the culture-change process is then explored in detail in subsequent chapters.

Senn-Delaney Leadership Process for Culture Change

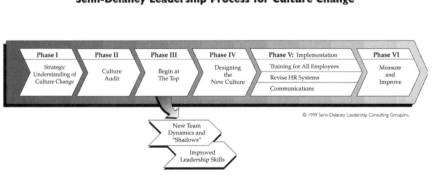

Figure 4

Phase I:
Strategic Understanding of Culture Change

The Strategic Understanding of Culture Change is the important first step that helps an organization see the impact of culture on organizational performance. It is useful here to educate management on what culture is, where it comes from, how it impacts performance, and the overall process for culture change. It is also important at this initial stage to begin a general discussion about what changes are happening in their industry and why the culture needs to change.

Since change is a function of perceived need, Phase I is also a time to educate the entire senior management team on the overall principles of culture change and their role in reshaping it. Even though most managers expend a significant amount of their time and energy dealing with team dysfunction and cultural barriers, nowhere in their careers have they been taught the skills of shaping culture or creating a high-performance team.

It is important at this critical educational phase to examine examples of other companies who have gone through successful culture change. It is often useful to:

- Learn more about what culture is, how cultures are built, what the difference is between a strong and a weak culture
- Do some outside reading
- Have open and frank discussions about the need for personal change as well as team and organizational change
- Talk with CEOs or other senior executives from companies that have embarked upon a culture change process

Phase II:
The Culture Audit and Gap Analysis

Most well-designed change initiatives, including Total Quality Management and Reengineering, rely on benchmarking and best practices studies early on in the process. These activities define the magnitude of the opportunity and establish a starting point for measuring progress. Parallels exist in reshaping culture as well:

- What external competitive or marketplace forces are impacting our business?
- What is our internal readiness for change?
- How deep are issues of mistrust?
- How aligned is the senior team?
- What is the level of teamwork between departments?
- What are the key cultural barriers to change?
- What cultural and organizational changes are needed to support new competitive strategies or performance improvements?

These and other questions need to be fully answered and understood by those leading a culture change within an organization before the process begins.

The underlying cultural barriers to business improvements are not always obvious, and it is often difficult for those inside the organization to clearly see their own culture. That is why it is useful to take advantage of an outsider's view in analyzing and shaping corporate culture.

The process of taking a culture audit (a snapshot of the current culture) is not quite as straightforward as in the more technical benchmarking study. Since culture is a holistic concept, much like an ecosystem, the interrelationships between cultural behaviors are as meaningful as the individual behaviors themselves. The broader questions to be answered are "What's really going on here?" "What's the story?" and "What are the implications for successful organizational change?"

The story can best be visualized and described through a culture audit—an active process of one-on-one interviews, evaluations of current planning documents, assessment of existing HR policies, review of corporate history, and an understanding of the industry and its driving forces. Measurement tools such as the Corporate Culture Profile™ and Guiding Behaviors Inventory™ are also helpful in establishing a profile of the current culture and its strengths and weaknesses.

> *Phase III:*
> Implement Solutions

Do as we do, not as we say.

The notion that change must begin at the top is based on the premise that organizations are shadows of their leaders. For a culture-shift to truly take root, the top management team must become role models of the new cultural values and workplace behaviors.

It is both difficult and impractical to separate leadership development, teambuilding, and culture-shaping. In today's complex organization, leadership by necessity takes place in the context of a team; be it the CEO and senior team or a team at another level. In turn, values, habits, and collective behaviors of the team cast a shadow on all they touch, thus influencing the overall culture. In short, the organizational behaviors will shift only if individual and team behaviors shift. Ideally, this shift begins at the top, but a leader or a team at any level can cast a shadow that affects all those around and under them.

This stage requires introspection and self-assessment on the part of senior management. The CEO and each member of the senior management team must ask themselves the following:

- What role model do I present to the organization?
- What kind of shadow do I cast?
- Am I, as a member of the senior management team, in alignment with our new mission and values?
- What dysfunction do we have as a team at the top that can be seen in the organization (turf issues, etc.)?

Communication and teamwork barriers must first be overcome at the top. A clear vision of the new culture must be collectively developed and thoroughly understood at the senior-most level before it can be actively implemented and translated into the day-to-day policy and behavior changes necessary to shift a culture.

All too often, organizations hire training companies to implement employee-development programs, or change-management skills or quality improvement programs for middle managers, expecting that these programs will bring about the desired changes. And, all too often, nothing significant happens because it was not supported and role-modeled from the top.

To ensure cultural transformation, there must be a shift in the behavior of the senior management team. It is absolutely critical to establish leadership alignment and role models at the top. The senior management team needs to interact and communicate in ways that model the new desired culture. It is during this phase that senior management commit to becoming true champions of the new culture and shift their own behaviors first—before they ask others to adopt the new culture.

Ideally, the central activity of Phase III is a high-impact, off-site retreat where members of the senior team better understand the strengths and weaknesses of the corporate culture as well as the senior team's internal working dynamics, and together explore their roles as leaders of a new, high-performance culture.

As the senior team begins to exhibit new levels of teamwork, openness, communication, and overall leadership, it begins to truly champion the culture-change process.

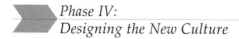

Phase IV:
Designing the New Culture

Deciding on the new culture helps the organization identify a new set of guiding behaviors that will allow the company to be even more successful in a changing business environment. In addition, it is important to develop a clear vision for the organization that will easily communicate, to all employees, who the organization is, where the organization is, and what is important.

This phase involves a careful examination of the organization's strategy and structure by the senior management team; it is their responsibility to develop a new cultural model and to define those values and behaviors that are consistent with the overall business strategy. This will include identifying those current values and behaviors that should be maintained, those which should be discouraged, and those which need to be developed.

This new cultural model must be consistent with the overall strategic and business plans while addressing the competitive pressures from the business environment. It should present clear benefits for the company as a whole, for individual employees, and for stockholders. The most effective cultural ingredients will be realistic, easily communicated to all levels of the organization, and capable of implementation through training and changes in various systems and structures.

The bottom-line question is, "Will these newly defined winning behaviors improve our competitive advantage?"

Phase V: Implementation

Implementation focuses on the activities of training, revising HR systems, and communication, each of which is crucial to the implementation of the new culture. Culture-change workshops, similar to the session developed for the senior team, can be developed for all employees so they can have a meaningful experience of the new culture. In these special, highly interactive workshops, new behaviors and expectations are not only discussed, but lived.

It is also important to review and revise the HR systems and policies so they are aligned with the new winning behaviors. Communication also plays a critical part in the overall shifting of the culture, and multiple formats for communicating to employees, customers, shareholders, the board of directors, vendors and suppliers, and even the families of employees, need to be developed and implemented.

Phase VI: Measurement and Ongoing Improvement

The culture of an organization and the behaviors of managers can be measured just like a budget or sales plan. Measurement, feedback, and continuous improvement are critical to culture change. Cultural alignment is a continuous process, not a series of static events, as changing business conditions will continue to impact the organization. Experience has shown that the process of shaping a new culture throughout a firm takes approximately two to three years. And that's with an active culture-change program!

Follow-up seminars are useful in reinforcing the new ways of thinking and working and should be implemented on an ongoing basis. Regular communications should be sent to all employees to share the progress and reinforce the momentum of the culture shift.

Several methods can be used to assist in the evaluation and feedback process. A tracking system can measure where the cultural gaps exist (those disparities between where an organization is and where it wants to be). Specially designed feedback instruments should be implemented on a regular basis. One of the best tools for measuring the shift in culture is a Guiding Behaviors Inventory™. This powerful tool is developed around the values and behaviors necessary for the new culture and provides valuable insight into the level of acceptance of the new culture. Feedback gives management a basis for further development and implementation of the desired culture change. (See Chapter 11 for more information about the 360° as a feedback and measurement tool.)

All of these processes were utilized in reshaping one of the most embedded kinds of cultures, that of a telephone company.

Bell Atlantic: A Success Story of Change Management

> Bell Atlantic is a change-management success story — a much touted hero that slashed service installation time from 16 days to 8 hours and has begun to win back customers from alternate-access carriers.

Before the breakup of AT&T in 1984, the Bell System was a classic example of how a corporate culture can evolve to successfully complement the strategies and organizational structures of a company. Because the Bell System developed and flourished in a highly regulated, monopolistic environment, its corporate culture adapted to meet those conditions. The organization was highly structured and bureaucratic with lifetime employment the social contract between company and employees. Also, being the only game in town had created an atmosphere that was far from customer-driven, although they were highly focused on customer service as they defined it. To standardize procedures and ensure reliable telephone service, a book of practices and procedures (known as "BST" or "the Practice") was created and followed religiously by employees as they responded to business and customer problems. In fact, if it wasn't in the "BST," it simply wasn't done.

While, in today's highly competitive world, that situation sounds like a design for failure, we must remember that it was a regulated monopoly, and this was the culture that best fit that environment. As a result, the United States had the finest, most reliable, and ubiquitous telephone service in the world.

When Ray Smith took over as the chairman and CEO of Bell Atlantic, he immediately recognized that he needed to drastically change its culture while implementing new competitive strategies at the same time. Smith saw three primary areas that needed to change:

- **Individual Accountability**—People were feeling victimized by divestiture, with too much finger-pointing and blaming. There were too many excuses and not enough proactive work on improving processes and performance. It was a classic entitlement mind-set that would not cut it in the new game

- **Turf Issues**—Smith also felt that they operated too much in what he called "stovepipes" (territorial groups that saw themselves as internally competitive rather than mutually supportive). The old joke was Pennsylvania (Bell) would celebrate if New Jersey (Bell) lost a rate case, even though they were both a part of Bell Atlantic. In order to truly compete in a global economy, the new Bell Atlantic couldn't act as six or seven separate state organizations or as separate functional areas. They had to become a more unified, effective operation

- **Bias-for-Action**—Less Bureaucracy—It was also clear that, no matter what shifts took place to improve the business, an overall sense of urgency needed to be embedded in all

employees. Things had to get done faster, with fewer com-
mittees, fewer meetings, shorter reviews, lower-level sign-
offs, and fewer people in the decision cycle

Smith began the change process by defining a set of principles he called the "Obligations of Leadership." He believed these
principles were the foundation necessary to transform the company into a successful competitor in the rapidly changing
telecommunications and information industry. While many of
the managers agreed with him on the changes needed and the
new behaviors defined in the Obligations of Leadership, the
change wasn't happening as rapidly as necessary. Like many
other CEOs trying to bring about change, he was frustrated by
its slow pace.

Bell Atlantic's experience was common to many organizations.
Shifting organizational habits is not easy, and merely talking about
it doesn't do it. People and organizations shift as a result of deeper
insights that come from experience. Smith realized that in order for
people to truly understand what he was saying, they had to experience it. Without that experience, the principles would remain
abstract concepts.

Being a visionary leader as well as an accomplished amateur
actor and playwright, Smith quickly made the connection between
Bell Atlantic and a play. He could easily see that a great play is really
only words on paper until the emotion and drama of the cast brings
it to life for the audience. In this case, the cast was the senior management team, and the audience the 80,000-plus employees of Bell
Atlantic.

With this new understanding of what was needed, an off-site
seminar was developed to give the senior team a shared experience
of the new culture. The Bell Atlantic officers spent three days in an
environment of increased accountability, trust, open communication, feedback, listening, and teamwork. It was just the experience
they needed. Just as it's impossible to really understand the culture
of a foreign country from reading a book, it's not feasible for people to comprehend a new corporate culture just by talking or reading about it. They have to experience it.

At the end of the retreat, many said "Aha! Now we understand
what Ray's been talking about!" They decided they wanted everyone

to experience this new culture, and to give them a guide, they created The Bell Atlantic Way, which included the values, behaviors, and philosophies they felt were the necessary foundations of the new culture. The Bell Atlantic Way became the guideline for conducting their business internally and externally. It is their code of conduct, a statement describing their new culture.

THE BELL ATLANTIC WAY BEHAVIORS

Our Responsibilities:

As Bell Atlantic employees, we share the responsibility to fully support our company's vision and the goals and strategies that will take us there. Therefore we must

▶ **Team Play.** This means that I constantly ask the questions "Who is Bell Atlantic?" "What is my team's purpose, and does that meet the requirements of customers, employees, shareowners, or communities?" Also, I do not foster internal competition. I focus my energy on new ways to create a win for the entire team.

▶ **Accept Accountability.** This means asking "What more can I do to get the results?" rather than looking for reasons why something did not get done. Accountable people look for ways to get the job done.

▶ **Empower.** I empower people when I trust them to do the job and do it well. I give them the authority and the resources they need to do their best, and I offer support and coaching to help them through.

▶ **Care About and Recognize Others.** This means I truly care about the personal and professional well-being of my colleagues, and I go out of my way to recognize their achievements and make them feel appreciated and valuable.

▶ **Listen and Be Here Now.** This means that when I am with someone, I care about what they have to say. I put other thoughts out of my mind so that I can "Be Here Now" with that person.

▶ **Encourage Risk.** I get outside of the "9 Dots" (outside of my comfort zone) to solve a problem even if I am not sure what the results will be. I show the members of my team that the only way to lose is by not trying to win.

▶ **Focus on Priority Issues.** I prioritize my time so that I take care of my "blue chips" first. I trust other members of my team with those things I don't have time to take care of myself.

Competitive success is about change. It is about being willing to challenge the status quo—the old methods—while being open to listen to any idea without being defensive, protective, or insecure. It's working in groups to make things better, having a big-picture focus, and looking at what's best for the whole company, rather than just an individual function. Those elements were embedded in The Bell Atlantic Way and allowed them to develop strategies to successfully compete in the telecommunications market.

Smith stated:

> *"Developing a culture of teamwork and accountability — The Bell Atlantic Way — has given us a foundation that allowed our restructuring and helped us compete in the new marketplace."*

The following chapters will guide you through the phases of culture change. Each of the processes has been successfully used by dozens of clients to shift critical behaviors in their culture.

5

PHASE I: STRATEGIC UNDERSTANDING OF CORPORATE CULTURE

Hewlett Packard posts record profits—DEC continues to struggle.
K-Mart is sluggish—Wal-Mart's growth continues.
Federal Express soars—U.S. Postal Service lags.
GE success continues—Westinghouse works at change.

Rarely does the performance of a company live up to the potential depicted in its organizational charts, strategic plans, or mission statements. The difference in performance from plan to reality is often significant and has been the speculation of countless articles and books on motivation, leadership, management skills, and other elements of the "soft" side of business.

But, are these elements really soft? While a business plan may look concrete with all of its facts and spreadsheets, it's actually an abstraction. It is an idea for the future and has no real existence in the organization or reality in the marketplace. The corporate culture, however, is a living, breathing dynamic force that has a life of its own, operating independently of all plans and projections, yet determining the success or failure of those plans.

THE BUSINESS OF CULTURE

The notion that the business performance of an organization is dependent upon a set of organizational behaviors that are often subjective and intangible is not new. These intangibles, which are far harder to measure than number of shipments or return on equity, are often the key factors in one organization's success compared with the success of another. The difference between success and failure in the business world can often be attributed to a limited set of organizational characteristics that combine to produce the corporate culture.

In a study of more than 200 companies reported in their important book *Corporate Culture and Performance*, John P. Kotter and James L. Heskett describe how shared values and unwritten rules can profoundly enhance economic success or, conversely, lead to failure to adapt to changing markets and environments.

THE ECONOMICS AND SOCIAL COSTS OF LOW-PERFORMANCE CULTURES (TWELVE-FIRM AVERAGE FOR 1977–1988)	Without Performance-Enhancing Cultures (%)	With Performance-Enhancing Cultures (%)
Revenue Growth	166	682
Employment Growth	36	282
Stock Price Growth	74	901
Tax Base (Net Income) Growth	1	756

Source: *Corporate Culture and Performance*, John P. Kotter and James L. Heskett. Used with permission.

According to Kotter and Heskett,

> *Strategy is simply a logic for how to achieve movement in some direction. The beliefs and practices called for in a strategy may be compatible with a firm's culture, or they may not. When they are not, a company usually finds it difficult to implement the strategies successfully.*

If culture supports the strategy of the organization and if agreement exists among members of the company about the importance of specific, high-performance values, the culture is said to be strong. In a company with a strong culture, you can feel the human energy that flows from aligned, committed employees. If little agreement exists, the culture is weak. In a company with a weak culture, the available energy is fragmented and often dissipated through conflicting agendas, blaming, and unclear communication.

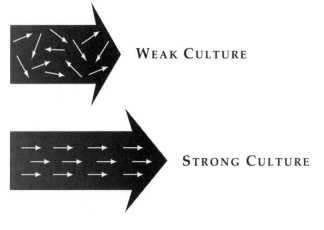

Figure 5.1

To the leaders of a company, corporate culture represents a powerful force that with the proper attention and leadership tools, can be focused and managed for the good of the company and its employees. In their book, *Corporate Cultures*, Terrence E. Deal and Allen A. Kennedy emphasize that effective corporate culture helps organizations and people be more productive:

> *A strong culture is a system of informal rules that spells out how people are to behave most of the time. By knowing what exactly is expected of them, employees will waste little time in deciding how to act in a given situation. In a weak culture, on the other hand, employees waste a good deal of time just trying to figure out what they should do and how they should do it. The impact of a strong culture on productivity is amazing. In the extreme, we estimate that a company can gain as much as one to two hours of productive work per employee per day!*

There are countless examples of how corporate culture impacts the profitability and efficiency of a business. In the manufacturing sector, the Toyota system of lean manufacturing and just-in-time inventory is possible only because a strong culture of trust has been built and nurtured. On the surface, it is as simple as everyone, from the chief executive to the shift worker, trusting one another to tell the truth, keep their word, and work toward a common objective, all the time. An economic model of trust (or lack of it) would look like this:

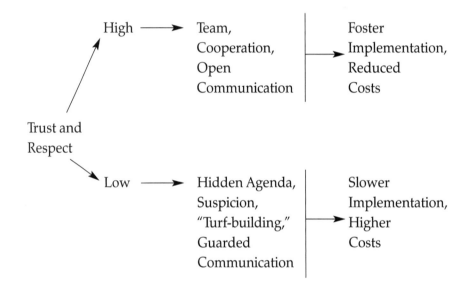

Trust and Respect

High → Team, Cooperation, Open Communication | Foster Implementation, Reduced Costs

Low → Hidden Agenda, Suspicion, "Turf-building," Guarded Communication | Slower Implementation, Higher Costs

One way to identify culture is to look at healthy versus unhealthy behaviors or habits in the organization. Are any of the following familar to you?

From **Ineffectual Organizational Habits** (old culture)	*To* **High-Performance Behaviors** (desired culture)
• We-they/win-lose internal competitiveness	• Collaborative, win-win internally in order to compete externally
• Resistance to change	• Embrace and help create change
• Decisions made in my own best interest	• Decisions made to support the broader good of the total organization
• I'm the boss, I have the answers and make the decisions	• I'm a leader who brings out the best in everyone
• Excessive time complaining about regulators, the changing market, and other things I don't like	• No time wasted on "givens," a focus on the future
• Blaming and excuses to cover up shortfalls	• A no-excuses, can-do attitude
• A "not-invented-here," shoot-down-new-ideas mind-set	• Learning and exploring new ideas to better the business
• Close to the vest, disclose as little as possible	• Openness and trust, open communication
• Assume negative motives about the company, other functions, and other people	• Assume best of intentions, all doing the best they can
• Talk to employees only when necessary to let them know when they made a mistake (i.e., leave alone and then "Zap")	• Provide a continual flow of appreciative and constructive coaching
• Autocratically direct everyone else and maintain tight control	• Encourage, empower, develop, delegate
• Worry, in a constant state of stress and apprehension	• Healthy mind-set, creative, innovative
• Risk-averse, avoid mistakes at all costs	• Bias for action and sense of urgency
• Delayed decisions	• Prudent and innovative change
• Distracted, preoccupied, non-listening	• Focused, present, hearing beyond the words
• Negative energy and attitude	• Positive energy and attitude

While Detroit sees the development as a major accomplishment of two to three productivity improvement ideas per employee per year, the average within Toyota is 30 to 40! Different cultures; different results in terms of global market share growth (or decline).

The economic importance of corporate culture is especially evident in the service industry. Those who lead service businesses know that the two key costs of service are staff turnover and customer turnover. Staff turnover results in excessive recruiting costs, training costs, and lost selling time. Customer turnover increases those costs associated with getting new customers, such as advertising, discounting, and special promotions.

If you've ever been to Harrod's Food Halls in London, or a Nordstrom store anywhere in the U.S., you will see people truly being served, and waiting in line for the privilege!

What prompts employees in one service company to be courteous, friendly, and responsive, while in a different company offering the same merchandise, to be surly, bored, abrupt, and hard to get a hold of? The different economics of these two examples lies in the difference in the corporate culture in terms of dignity and fulfillment provided to employees.

WHAT IS CORPORATE CULTURE AND WHERE DOES IT COME FROM?

In the broadest sense, corporate culture refers to the personality of the organization, the shared beliefs, and the written and unwritten policies and procedures that determine the ways in which the organization and its people behave and solve business problems. Culture provides the meaning, direction, and clarity (the human glue) that mobilizes the collective energy of a corporation toward goals and accomplishments.

Corporate culture is a composite of the following:

- Shared Values–*What we think is important*
- Beliefs–*How we think things should be done*
- Behaviors–*The habitual patterns of the organization*
- Heroes–*The people who personify our corporate culture*
- Systems–*Our written and unwritten policies and procedures*

More simply put, it's "the way we do things around here."

In order to use corporate culture as a tool in business improvement and organizational change, it is important to understand how a culture is formed and what the major ingredients are in the development of a corporate culture.

An individual's personality is the result of genetic inheritance, environmental influences, and current thought processes. Similarly, a corporation's culture is determined by everything that touches it: its industry, workers, leaders, history, customers, suppliers, stockholders, regulatory agencies, and community.

Corporate culture is created through the interaction of the critical Key Determinants of Culture:

- Corporate History
  - Leadership Style
    - Industry and Environment
      - Region
        - Employee Base
          - Key Organizational Tasks

The following model shows these Key Determinants of Culture and how they interact to form the corporate culture.

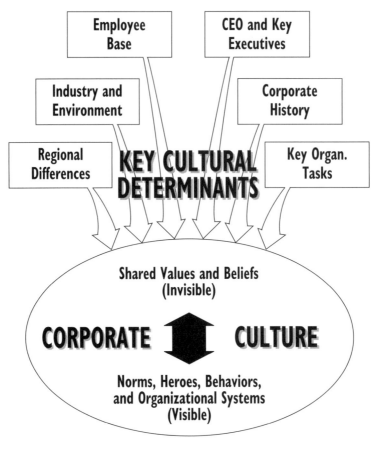

Figure 5.2

Every organization develops its own cultural distinctions based on these key influencing factors:

Corporate History—Nordstrom began as a shoe store. That has greatly influenced its culture. In a well-run, service-oriented shoe store, customers get a lot of special attention. The salesperson measures the customer's feet, goes to get various styles and sizes of shoes, and puts them on the customer's feet. Since most shoe salespeople work on commission, a strong sales consciousness also exists.

From that base, Nordstrom began to add apparel to become a

department store, but the shoe-store traditions carried forward. Is it any wonder that people marvel at how a Nordstrom salesperson will run around the store to find items to complete an outfit?

Apple Computer was begun by two young entrepreneurs whose total focus was to create a personal computer that was easy to operate and user-friendly. In contrast, IBM, a data-tabulating company focused on large mainframes, sold to more sophisticated information officers. IBM had to rely upon another young maverick, Bill Gates, to create a PC operating system, yet even today, Apple's Macintosh operating system is widely recognized as more user-friendly than the Windows operating system.

Unfortunately for Apple, its future is uncertain because the maverick culture that developed people-friendly systems wasn't ideally suited to operate in the size and scope of the industry today. They have failed to make the transition from a creation culture to a large-scale delivery culture.

Leadership Style—The most consistent finding from all research done on corporate culture is the following:

Organizations become shadows of their leaders.

In every organization, there are the shadows cast by current leaders and the ghosts of former leaders. In examining a culture, it is usually easy to determine the impact of current leaders as well as previous leaders. Have the leaders been visionary, restrictive, participative, behind the times, open, secretive, entrepreneurial, status quo, innovative, family-oriented, or conservative?

Ross Perot, founder of EDS, left IBM because it was too slow-moving and bureaucratic. He had a forceful personality with a military mind-set, and was very hard-working, goal-oriented, and principled. Many years later, that hard-working, aggressive quality can still be seen at EDS as well as Perot Systems.

Hewlett Packard had a team-based culture decades before it was the thing to do. That was simply an outgrowth of William Hewlett's and David Packard's philosophy of having smaller team-based units no matter how much the firm grew. They established the HP Way, a set of cultural values that still serves the corporation well today.

Industry and Environment—The characteristics of an industry can create dramatically different cultures, such as a defense contractor compared to an advertising agency. In their dealings with the federal government, defense contractors have to adhere to stringent sets of specifications, rules, and regulations. This environment tends to attract analytical, thorough, and deliberate people who thrive in an intensely structured milieu. These people hire other people who can handle regulations and ensure conformity to standards; they do business with suppliers who follow regulations and procedures. Gradually, the corporate personality grows more distinct and people who do not fit the mold opt out or are forced out.

Advertising agencies exist in a totally different environment. They require fast-paced people with a high sense of urgency and the ability to make quick decisions based on both consumer data and emotional appeal. They make heroes of people with creative flair and a sense of style and abhor bureaucracies and regulations.

Region—Is the firm global or local? Is it headquartered in the Silicon Valley, inner city, rural agricultural area, Pacific Rim, sun belt, Bible belt, university area, or midwestern suburbs? Wal-Mart has that folksy feeling, in part, because it's based in Bentonville, Arkansas, and not New York City.

Employee Base—The demographics of the work force play a key role in creating a culture. Some examples are young, fast-food part-timers, well-educated information workers; skilled production workers, and volunteers. Are employees technically oriented, creative, risk-averse people, skilled, unskilled, female or male? Retail cultures differ from nuclear utilities, in part, because one has a significant percentage of technical people with engineering or science degrees, and the other has very few.

Key Organizational Tasks—What is the primary product or service? Is it software programming, engineering, retail sales, logging, airport transportation, machinery operation, education, or manufacturing? Key tasks reflect the kind of employee base, the nature of industry, leadership style, and other determinants of culture.

Imagine the corporate cultures that might result from these two scenarios:

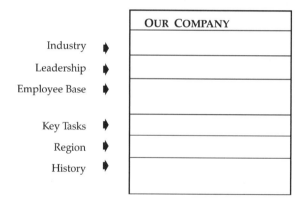

	COMPANY #1	COMPANY #2
Industry ▶	High technology	Retail
Leadership ▶	Entrepreneurial	Finance background
Employee Base ▶	Young, well-educated, salaried professionals	Mostly hourly employees
Key Tasks ▶	Programming	Merchandising

In order to understand your own culture, just give some thought to how it is influenced by the founders, industry, current leaders, employee base, and key tasks.

	OUR COMPANY
Industry ▶	
Leadership ▶	
Employee Base ▶	
Key Tasks ▶	
Region ▶	
History ▶	

VALUES AND BELIEFS: THE INNER FABRIC OF CULTURE

Key cultural determinants interact in various ways to create the inner fabric of corporate culture: the Shared Values and Beliefs. Values are the important philosophical underpinnings of the organization that spell out what is important within the company. Values often include integrity, concern for employees, and a high service ethic, but may also include such business practicalities as loyalty and respect for position.

Beliefs refer to "the way we are supposed to be around here" and include both empowering and limiting beliefs such as:

- We should all work as a team
- Keep your head down and don't make waves
- People should follow rules
- Follow the chain of command
- Have an open-door policy
- Managers are paid to make decisions
- Hourly employees can't be trusted with financial data
- Fair pay for a fair day's work
- People need to be motivated
- It is not safe to admit a mistake

When values and beliefs are shared by a group of people who work together to accomplish an overall objective, they exert a tremendous power over the attitudes and behaviors of all employees. They become a powerful set of unwritten ground rules that guide daily decisions and actions. These shared values and beliefs can be so strong that individuals coming into an organization with a different set of values and beliefs may find it difficult to fit in. Sometimes the person faces a choice of adapting to the rules of the game or leaving the company.

The values that members of an organization share create a template for corporate and individual behavior. Some companies see their corporate values as a source of competitive advantage, allowing the organization and its members to react quickly and decisively to business events and competitive pressures.

James Burke, former chairman of Johnson & Johnson, believes that the Johnson & Johnson Credo, their statement of shared values, allowed individuals to react swiftly during the Tylenol-tampering incident without wasting valuable time on the chain of command or seeking formal approval. Lower-level managers made the decision to pull millions of dollars of suspect product off the shelves because that action was consistent with the company's long-held values.

JOHNSON & JOHNSON CREDO

- We believe our first responsibility is to the doctors, nurses and patients, to mothers, to fathers and all others who use our products and services.

- We are responsible to our employees, the men and women who work with us throughout the world.

- We are responsible to the communities in which we live and work and to the world community as well.

- Our final responsibility is to our stockholders. Business must make a sound profit.

Source: Excerpts from the Credo in Johnson & Johnson Press Kit.

Many organizations are beginning to recognize the power of shared values and make them part of their reward and recognition system. Jack Welch, CEO of GE, represents the new breed of corporate leader who passionately believes in the importance of the organization's values. In a recent interview, he stated:

> *In an environment with values, everyone can create a win. Values are a key to our success at GE. Our first value for GE is to "Create a clear, simple, reality-based, customer-focused vision and be able to communicate it straightforwardly to all constituencies."*

BEHAVIORAL NORMS, HEROES, AND ORGANIZATIONAL SYSTEMS

While it is difficult to see values and beliefs, it is easy to see their effects in the organization's behavioral norms, financial and human resource systems, the behavior of managers and employees, and hero stories. This is the visible part of culture and the behavioral norms can be seen in the style and pace of meetings, frequency and importance of planning sessions, work habits and hours, communication between different levels and functions of the organization, style of dress and office decoration, and level of cooperation versus competition. Values and beliefs are also formalized into the organization's systems: personnel policies, procedures, rules, project-review systems, budget-approval policies, and other systems.

Another way the organization's culture is displayed is through hero stories. The behaviors and actions that become legend within a company are strong indications of what the company believes is important. However, behavioral norms, organizational systems, and stories the organization tells are more than just the visible clues to the organization's culture. They also reinforce and perpetuate the culture, both positively and negatively.

People are shaped by the behavioral norms that surround them and are guided by the systems created by the organization. The hero stories that are repeated to new members of an organization introduce them to the corporate culture. Some companies do this formally as a way of shaping behavior: Wal-Mart still actively promotes stories about Sam Walton as an example of positive Wal-Mart cultural values. Other organizations do it more informally, such as many of the Silicon Valley companies that continue to tell stories about the early days and the creativity of founding heroes.

THE SECRETS OF RESHAPING CULTURE

Even when one accepts the fact that culture can make or break any change initiative (or any company, for that matter), the question is, can culture be changed, and if so, how?

Reshaping culture is similar to changing the lifelong habits and behaviors of a person. It is not easy to stop smoking or permanently lose weight, but people do. It is not easy to break down the walls between departments, but organizations can become more boundary-less.

The good news is that more organizations are recognizing the need to shift culture and are working at it. The bad news is, like losing weight, most companies make too little progress too slowly or lose and then regain more fat than before. Our research and experience have taught us what it takes to successfully reshape a culture and why most companies fail.

Principle #1
ORGANIZATIONS ARE SHADOWS OF THEIR LEADERS

We learned this lesson early in our history. J.L. Hudson, a division of the Dayton Hudson Corporation in Detroit, asked us to help them work on improving customer service in their stores in the late 70s. They wanted to be more like Nordstrom. We piloted the process in six stores, working with the store managers. We had mixed success. Some stores had measurable increases in service levels and increased market share, while others didn't. In fact, the results were almost directly proportional to our success in shifting the store manager's focus from operations to service, and his/her management style. It demonstrated how the leader's cast of influence crossed the store. This is what we would later call "the shadow of the leader."

We concluded our mixed success was a result of starting at the wrong level in the organization. We found this out in an interesting way. When we asked sales associates why they weren't more attentive or friendlier to customers, they would, in different ways say, "Who's friendly and attentive to me?" When we asked their department managers the same question, we got the same answer. That continued on up through the assistant store manager, the store manager, the district manager, the vice president of stores, and on up to the executive committee. We concluded that fixing the stores was similar to family therapy; you have to include the parents. Later, when the CEO of The Broadway Department Stores in California asked if we would develop a customer service process for them, we politely said, "Only if we can begin with the executive committee." That led to several consecutive years of increased sales and market share for The Broadway.

All too often, leaders in an organization will kick off meetings about quality, but not develop quality measures or improvements in their own work. They will announce reengineering, but not reengineer their own jobs. They will approve of training programs dealing with changes such as culture, but not attend to or visibly work on changing themselves.

Principle #2
You Can't Create What You Can't Define

No company would think of operating without an income state-ment, a balance sheet, or some sort of budgeting process. Those things define the quantitative goals for the organization and let everyone know when they are on target. Yet, most organizations have no clear definition of culture and no way of measuring cul-tural ingredients. Detailed cultural definitions in the form of val-ues and guiding behaviors are a cornerstone of the change process.

Principle #3
Define the Gap

How much change is needed and in what areas? Not only do orga-nizations have income statements, balance sheets, and budgets, but they have variance reports and periodic audits to see if they are on target. Few companies do an effective job of auditing their cul-ture and measuring the gap.

- What is the degree of change readiness?
- How deep is the resistance to change?
- How easy will it be to create cross-organizational solutions?
- Will the historical hierarchy and level consciousness pre-vent the use of competency-based versus position-based teams?

Principle #4
Get an Outside View of Your Cultural Strengths
and Weaknesses

There is an interesting saying that relates to culture: "We don't know who discovered water, but we're pretty sure it wasn't a fish." Understanding a culture is a similar phenomenon. It's like water to a fish; they don't know what it is because they are immersed in it. The same is true with corporate culture. When people are surrounded by it every day, they don't see it. It's like living in a noisy city: Pretty soon you don't hear the traffic. This phenomenon has been referred to as "familiarity blindness" or "cultural trance."

Principle #5
CHANGE IS A FUNCTION OF PERCEIVED NEED

In a personal interview, Lee Iacocca described to us how and why Chrysler got serious about culture change:

> *We bought American Motors, which was a big merger. We had to integrate them at the same time the market (Wall Street) crashed 508 points. It all happened within two weeks. And that awakened us. And it didn't take six months to say, "We're going to die if we don't change."*

> *We had to change major habits in our culture. This country was built on the rugged individualism that characterized the 1930s, '40s, and '50s. Everything was top-down, as in the army or the Catholic Church–the great hierarchies of the world. The word comes down from above. That's the way the hierarchy of business was done. That's a tough culture to change. But easy or not, you have to change. We did it at Chrysler. We began with off-site meetings, we now call "Core Sessions." We started with our officers, and then we took the training down into the organization. We immersed our managers in the culture change.*

It is important to begin to educate the entire employee body about culture, the need for fundamental change in American business today, the need for change within our company, and the importance of culture in the overall change process. As much as possible, this should be a fact-based message, with a balance of information about both potential threat as well as future opportunity. The danger of communicating the need for change using only the fear of loss of jobs is that it can often, especially in unempowered, more hierarchical cultures, drive employees into a foxhole mentality.

As one middle manager recently described it:

For the past month all we've heard from senior management is WE need to change, or else! We hear lots about competition eating our lunch, how we are "bloated" and not cost effective, how we've got to get rid of "dead wood" employees who aren't pulling their weight! There's no opportunity in these messages; no picture for the future. As a result, it's easy to see why many employees have gotten into a "hunker down" attitude where everybody tends to lie low, be as inconspicuous as possible, don't make any waves, and for certain don't volunteer for anything that could make you stand out!

Resistance to change in companies today occurs because people in the organization don't see a compelling need for change and, therefore, don't have a sense of urgency. One client of ours, a large regional phone company, established a "Competitive Newsletter." In it, they printed every piece of news on how technology was changing and how others were moving to take their market. They went to great lengths to communicate that they could either shrink as an old-line phone company or get their costs and culture in line and be a winner in the new information age.

Principle #6
BEHAVIORAL CHANGE OCCURS AT THE EMOTIONAL, NOT INTELLECTUAL LEVEL

Meaningful change in the beliefs, habits, and behaviors of people often comes as a result of significant emotional events. It rarely comes from reading a book or attending a lecture. Events like a health crisis, a divorce, or the birth of a child will cause someone to look at the world through a different set of eyes. The same is true for organizations. IBM, Sears, and other organizations are in the process of remaking themselves. This probably wouldn't be happening without the crises they face.

Given the importance of crisis as a triggering activity, how does a company reshape its culture without a looming crisis? We have found that people can be drawn toward a positive vision of the future that is both compelling and emotionally rewarding. This is understandable in the light of the fact that deep-seated values and beliefs reside in the heart or the gut, not in the head.

Statements of values hang on the walls but don't live in the hearts of employees because this rule is so often violated. We have found that unless a senior team arrives at their values through a specially designed team process, preferably an off-site retreat that creates a positive, shared, emotional experience, these values won't be internalized. Unless the values are internalized by the senior team, neither the understanding nor the commitment will be deep enough. Habits and culture can only be changed through an insightful, personal experience, not an intellectual seminar or lecture.

Principle #7
CULTURE CHANGE REQUIRES A
FEEDBACK-RICH COACHING ENVIRONMENT

Reinforcement is critical to behavior change. Annual reviews of performance are not adequate to support culture change. We've asked hundreds of groups of executives in our seminars if they receive enough useful, appreciative, or constructive feedback to help them with behavior change. Not once has a group said yes.

In our off-site Executive Leadership Workshops, participants are often shocked to find that they receive more useful feedback that helps them improve their leadership skills during a 30- minute interactive exercise, than they have in the past 5 to 10 years of their careers.

Culture change requires day-to-day ongoing coaching where people are appreciated for new behaviors and supportively and constructively coached when they are violating cultural conventions. In addition to active coaching, other more formal reinforcement mechanisms, like 360° feedback and peer-review programs, must be set in place.

Principle #8
LEADERSHIP SKILLS AND CULTURE CHANGE WORK BEST
IN NATURAL WORK GROUPS

A few years ago, we were asked to review the culture-change efforts of a large corporation. It had spent millions in training and education and hadn't made a dent in the old hierarchical, command-and-control culture. Like many organizations, it had set up a sophisticated, in-house university. They offered a wide variety of topical courses on leadership, teambuilding, and culture, and they also sent selected executives off to some of the finer business school programs and leadership centers in the country.

The problem was, people who worked shoulder-to-shoulder on real issues rarely went to the classes together; therefore, they didn't have a common language nor were they able to reinforce one another's learning. Since leadership and coaching take place within the context of a team, team-based training is vital to culture change.

Some years back we were not effective enough in communicating the importance of this rule. Because one client had such serious turf issues and because they historically had done their training by level of the organization, they began to rollout training horizontally to mixed groups of employees, all at the same organizational levels. Later we found that they weren't applying the concepts enough on the job. Because intact work groups had not had the same shared bonding experience, they didn't feel permission to coach one another on new ways of working together. When we switched to intact team training to reconnect them, the culture change dramatically accelerated.

ENSURING THE OUTCOMES WITH PURPOSE AND EMPOWERMENT

One of the most dramatic organizational changes we have seen was undertaken by Branch Banking & Trust Company (BB&T) of North Carolina, and led by its chairman, John Allison. BB&T was a regional bank that was growing at 8 percent per year in a market that was growing 10 percent, and it was rapidly losing market share, as well as its own confidence. What did it take to turn the organization around to one that averaged over 31 percent growth per year for over five consecutive years? According to Allison, overcoming resistance is mostly being fanatical about getting everyone aligned around a clear purpose and empowering people at all levels.

Allison and the employees of BB&T found that the secret for overcoming resistance and building an entirely new organization was culture change:

- Get absolutely clear about your real purpose as a business
- Achieve 100 percent buy-in to that purpose
- Empower employees at all levels to focus on purpose, not just goals
- Eliminate, in a caring manner, the resistors

According to Allison, this early experience had a profound and positive impact on his own personal life and the lives of all those employees who participated in the bank's purpose: "solving the financial problems of our customers."

Most senior managers forget that there is a basic conflict that occurs between management and employees that becomes accentuated during times of change. That conflict is the fundamental difference between management's financial focus and most employees' customer focus. Employees don't get nearly as excited about cost reduction as they do about solving a customer's problem. And many managers forget that the bottom line numbers they look at every day on spreadsheets come from the pockets of thousands of customers with whom they never interface.

One of the major problems during change is that much of the focus of management gets intensified on the financial objectives, which adds to the concern of employees that customers are going to get less service than before. These two different focuses are analogous to a pair of binoculars where each of the two eyepieces are focused on different scenes—it's easy to wind up with a splitting headache that way! Leaders of change must understand that their job is not to try and make both focuses the same, but to tie them together, like the cross-pieces of steel in a good pair of binoculars that keep each of the eyepieces aligned. This is possible by developing a higher purpose that all employees at all levels can buy into.

THE VALUE OF PURPOSE

A series of visionary, yet specific, purpose statements can help guide all employees during a large-scale change process. A Culture-Change Purpose should be a clear picture of the desired internal working environment during the change process. An example could be:

> *During this change process, we will engage the energy, excitement, and ideas of all our employees in such a healthy manner as to have open, honest dialogue, empowerment, accountability, and team-work become a part of our ongoing corporate culture.*

The development of a Business Purpose Statement is critical to providing human energy and vitality to the entire change process. Everyone needs a purpose to believe in. And very few of your employees will fully believe in and commit to "improved earnings per share" or "reduced costs and faster cycle time!" These are end results, not purposes. A purpose is something that gets people up in the morning and makes them feel good during the day, not just when the results are in! Look for your Vision and Purpose Statement in the things that really matter in your organization. For example, one of our clients, a toy manufacturer, expresses his Business Purpose Statement this way:

> **Making the world safer and even more fun for babies and children!**

By framing and committing to a Performance Objective, a Culture-Change Objective, and then developing an overall Business Purpose Statement, the entire organization can identify with a balanced set of outcomes for the change process.

Reader Activity

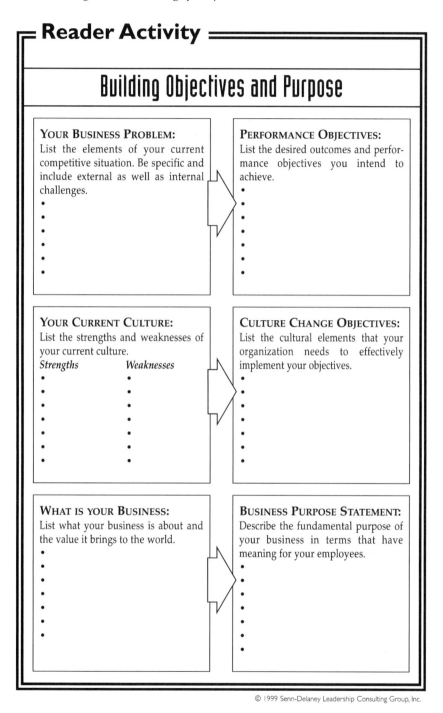

Building Objectives and Purpose

YOUR BUSINESS PROBLEM:
List the elements of your current competitive situation. Be specific and include external as well as internal challenges.
-
-
-
-
-
-

PERFORMANCE OBJECTIVES:
List the desired outcomes and performance objectives you intend to achieve.
-
-
-
-
-
-
-

YOUR CURRENT CULTURE:
List the strengths and weaknesses of your current culture.

Strengths   *Weaknesses*
-
-
-
-
-
-
-

CULTURE CHANGE OBJECTIVES:
List the cultural elements that your organization needs to effectively implement your objectives.
-
-
-
-
-
-

WHAT IS YOUR BUSINESS:
List what your business is about and the value it brings to the world.
-
-
-
-
-
-
-

BUSINESS PURPOSE STATEMENT:
Describe the fundamental purpose of your business in terms that have meaning for your employees.
-
-
-
-
-

6

PHASE II: CORPORATE CULTURE AUDIT

Without a clear picture of the current culture, it is impossible to understand the tremendous impact and influence that an organization's culture will have on the outcome of its business change initiatives. Embarking upon any change initiative without understanding the strengths and weaknesses of the current corporate culture is like pulling out of the driveway on a fabulous summer vacation that has been planned all winter, but then not checking the gas, oil level, or general condition of the car. It's a design destined to fail!

So how can we get a clear picture of our current corporate culture? This is not easy, since the existing culture is often invisible to those working inside the company. The underlying values, beliefs, and even the norms and policies and procedures that make up the current culture are so commonplace that cultural myopia becomes real. Too often, management aggressively defends "the way things are done around here" as being somehow perfect and certainly not a contributor to poor performance! The only way to determine the degree to which culture is a root -cause contributor is to develop an objective picture of the current corporate culture.

Even though this may be difficult for insiders, there are a number of ways to get clues:

• *What gets attention in conversations and in meetings?* If, for example, 90 percent of a typical management meeting is spent talking about reducing costs, and 10 percent is spent on how the customers are feeling, then you probably have more of a cost-driven than a customer-driven culture.

• *Notice people's behavior.* If you were to make up a list of behaviors that you see frequently, whether the behavior contributes to or detracts from the good of the company, what would be on the list? For example, if people in your culture tend to shoot down new ideas, pointing out why they will not work, then that would be a characteristic of your culture. Or, if people in your culture tend to openly appreciate each other, then that would describe your culture.

• *What are the hero stories?* As mentioned earlier, an equally influential part of the visible culture are the stories an organization tells. The behaviors and actions that become legend within a company are strong signals of the way things should be done around here! Who do people stand around and talk about with pride and respect? What behaviors do these people exhibit? Who gets applauded at meetings? What are the behaviors that warrant the applause? Within all strong cultures, the keen observer will find dozens of stories that clearly spell out the expectations the company has for its employees.

• *Ask "what if" questions.* In working with a large electric utility, we asked the senior team to imagine who in America could be their toughest competitor if they decided to go into their business, and how they would have to change to survive. The group picked Microsoft and Motorola and concluded that they would have to eliminate the bureaucracy, be far more open to change, and have a markedly higher bias for action.

• *Get fresh feedback.* Check with those who have "stranger's eyes." Ask the newest managers in the organization to describe what they notice in the culture that's different for them. What did they first notice as strengths and challenges? Do the same with longtime trusted vendors and any consultants working on projects within the organization. All can provide outside perspective.

An additional and even more direct way to understand your current culture is to get assistance in conducting a corporate culture audit. It is interesting to note that organizations regularly audit all aspects of financial performance. Since culture is such a strong determining factor in performance, why not audit it as well?

The Culture Audit

Culture audits basically take two forms: the subjective interview method, and the more objective questionnaire or profile method. Our recommendation is that both are important in gaining an understanding of a company's current culture. Together, they develop a more complete picture.

The interview methodology gives good rich information, filled with examples and feelings, but its subjective nature makes it hard to analyze or quantify the information. The quantifiable profile or questionnaire method delivers measurable data, but is without any real integrated meaning or contextual understanding. Together, however, they have a positive synergistic effect that helps paint a very complete and understandable picture of the strengths and weaknesses of the current culture.

While several "canned" profiles are available, it is advisable to develop one that is tailored specifically for an organization. While the pre-packaged materials may be slicker and somewhat less time-consuming to get completed, there is great value in developing, administering, and analyzing one specifically tailored for a company. Just by going through the process of deciding which questions to ask, the senior management team will learn about their corporate culture. And by implementing it, a leader will quickly learn the degree of openness, honesty, or self-confidence of the culture. And, even more important than the statistics, is the richness of the discussions that will occur as the group works through the summary together.

Our recommendation is that an outside expert in culture be retained to help the company develop and implement their culture audit. In many cases they are the best ones to conduct the interview portions, since in many cultures it is not necessarily "job healthy" to tell it like it is to insiders. And then, of course, there is the important area of confidentiality. An outside expert is also important when it comes to interpreting the information.

DEVELOPING A CULTURE AUDIT

A culture audit can be developed and a profile of the current culture established by conducting an active process of one-on-one interviews with all levels of the organization. Combined with an evaluation of the current planning documents, an assessment of the existing HR policies, a review of the corporate history, and an understanding of the industry and its driving forces, a company can then assess its cultural strengths and weaknesses.

In developing the questions and areas to explore, we recommend some of the following:

- What are the major strengths of this company?
- How well is this company prepared for the future?
- In what ways is this company vulnerable?
- Which areas in the organization tend to cooperate, and which ones don't?
- Is more effort spent on internal competition or external?
- When a goal or deadline is missed, or a result not accomplished, do people tend to make excuses and blame others, or are they highly accountable?
- Is it OK to make a mistake around here?
- Does the organization tend to be hierarchical and level conscious?
- Do people tend to have a strong work ethic? Is there any stress and burnout?
- What is our customer service really like?
- Does the culture tend to encourage new ideas or shoot them down?
- Are issues openly discussed in meetings or afterwards, in the hall?
- What are the current levels of trust and openness in the organization?

Additional informal and subjective approaches are also helpful in assessing culture. From a personal perspective it is helpful to

- Disengage yourself from your own view of the business

- Talk with employees with whom you would not normally interact
- Ask your spouse or friends for feedback about the company
- Make a list of company jokes: There is usually more truth than humor in them.

The answers to these questions will prepare the senior management team to begin an open and candid evaluation of the current culture and it's role in leading the performance improvement process.

CORPORATE CULTURE PROFILE™

One tool we have developed for use in our own organization to help clients get a handle on their culture is the Corporate Culture Profile. A group, usually beginning with the entire senior team, is asked to complete the profile. They mark their perceptions of the strength of a number of cultural traits on a scale, such as the one shown on page 76. The sample can be as small as the senior team or as large as the entire company. Within one multi-national organization, a Corporate Culture Profile was administered to a total of 1,000 employees from various levels in a dozen different countries.

The profiles shown in the following charts are representative of a large U.S. company in the energy industry. A look at the highest and lowest scores usually tells a story. In this case, the strengths are obvious. They are a high-integrity company of self-starters with high-performance expectations. They genuinely care about customers and service. The lowest scores are indicative of a regulated utility mindset: internally competitive, highly political, and bureaucratic. This company is struggling with change caused by deregulation and increasing competition and so far has done an ineffective job of communicating to their employees why they need to change, and after considerable downsizing, trust levels are low. It is interesting to note that this company is at the front end of a major organizational change process, and already they are encountering difficulties because of resistance to change, interdepartmental turf issues, and power struggles among division leaders.

Figure 6.1

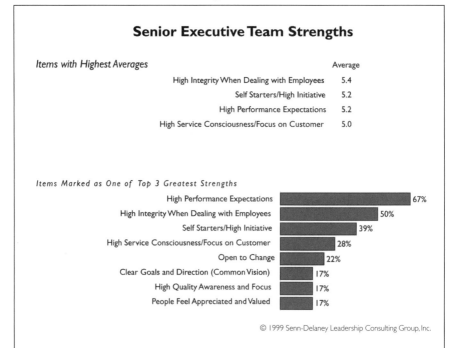

Figure 6.2

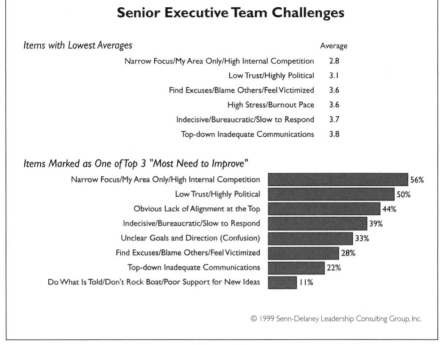

Figure 6.3

One-on-one interviews, focus groups, and an understanding of the industry and the company history can bring added life to the data. In the case of the utility, it had an older-generation management team with a solid work ethic, which helps explain the high-performance expectations score. Many managers had engineering or operations backgrounds, which created an internal operations culture versus an external marketing or customer focus. The organization had historically been functionally and/or geographically organized, and because they were a regulated monopoly, they didn't face outside competition. The combination led to a turf-oriented, internally competitive culture, characterized by them as "silos." Because their product had a very long life cycle (compared to computers) they were not used to change and tended to resist it. Since they had for many years been a lifetime employment firm, people played it safe and avoided conflict to stay in favor and move up the ladder. The result was a risk-averse, hierarchical, and boss-led culture.

The data from the culture-assessment interviews and the

Corporate Culture Profile was convincing enough evidence to management that they decided to move more aggressively on reshaping their culture to support their business change initiatives.

SOME OBSERVATIONS FROM CORPORATE CULTURE PROFILES

We have completed and analyzed hundreds of Corporate Culture Profiles™ (CCP) for organizations. Some of the more generic and the more interesting generalizations include:

- Stress levels and burnout (question 19) have been rising over the past five years. More people are feeling overwhelmed and dealing with balance-in-life issues.
- High stress levels are almost always accompanied by low scores in "appreciation" (question 17) and "high performance expected but not recognized" (question 15). Conversely, stress levels are almost never high when people feel appreciated, valued, and recognized.
- Classic older institutions, as could be expected, have less sense of urgency, more turf, more bureaucratic tendencies, and more blaming and excuses versus accountability. The CCP helps them measure progress as they shift these tendencies over time.
- Younger growing organizations tend to have a greater sense of urgency and innovation but still often have burnout and lack of feedback and appreciation.
- People's intentions are good. The score that is consistently highest is "High Performance Expectations" (question 8); i.e., people want to perform well and to win.

Every company's culture contains a story. When that story is understood and compared to current business realities, the shifts in behavior necessary to be most successful become obvious. This is true for a company, a department, or a work team. What's the story in your culture?

Take your own survey.

Describe Your Perception of Sample Company

#	Strengths	Always a Strength (7)	(6)	Sometimes Both (5)	(4)	(3)	Always a Challenge (2)	(1)	Challenges
1	People Clearly Understand Vision, Mission and Goals	○	○	○	○	○	○	○	People Are Unclear About Vision, Mission And Goals
2	Clear Alignment/Common Focus of Leadership at Top	○	○	○	○	○	○	○	Obvious Lack of Alignment at the Top
3	Two-Way Frequent Open Communications	○	○	○	○	○	○	○	Top-Down, Inadequate Communications
4	Flexible/Fluid/Empowered	○	○	○	○	○	○	○	Hierarchical/Boss Driven
5	High Quality Awareness and Focus	○	○	○	○	○	○	○	Quality Not a High Priority
6	High Service Consciousness/Focus on Customer	○	○	○	○	○	○	○	Low Service Consciousness/Lack of Focus on the Customer
7	Teamwork/Mutual Support and Cooperation	○	○	○	○	○	○	○	Narrow Focus/Turf Issues/We vs. They
8	High Performance Expectations	○	○	○	○	○	○	○	Low Performance Expectations
9	Self Starters/High Initiative	○	○	○	○	○	○	○	Need Direction/Low Initiative
10	Sense of Urgency/Bias for Action	○	○	○	○	○	○	○	Indecisive/Bureaucratic/Slow to Respond
11	People are Highly Accountable for Results and Actions	○	○	○	○	○	○	○	People Find Excuses/Blame Others/Feel Victimized
12	Open to Change	○	○	○	○	○	○	○	Resistant to Change
13	Encouraged to Innovate/Creativity Welcomed	○	○	○	○	○	○	○	Do What is Told/Risk Averse/Poor Support for New Ideas
14	High Levels of Feedback and Coaching	○	○	○	○	○	○	○	Infrequent or No Feedback and Coaching
15	High Performance is Recognized and Rewarded	○	○	○	○	○	○	○	High Performance is Expected But Not Recognized or Rewarded
16	Core Values and Ethics are Very Important	○	○	○	○	○	○	○	Values and Ethics Not Stressed or Tend to be Ignored
17	People Feel Appreciated and Valued	○	○	○	○	○	○	○	People Don't Feel Appreciated and Valued
18	High Trust/Openness Between People	○	○	○	○	○	○	○	Low Trust/Lack of Openness
19	Healthy/Fast Paced Environment	○	○	○	○	○	○	○	High Stress/Burnout Pace
20	Positive/Optimistic/Forgiving	○	○	○	○	○	○	○	Insecure/Fearful or Negative Environment
21	Focused/Balanced/Effective	○	○	○	○	○	○	○	Distracted/Overwhelmed/Inefficient
22	Respect for Diversity of Ideas and People	○	○	○	○	○	○	○	Lack of Respect for Diversity of Ideas and People

Fill out this survey yourself or have your team complete it.

Reader Activity

Culture and Its Implications

List the key strengths and weaknesses of your current culture as indicated in your culture profile. With your senior team, determine the possible implications these can have on your goals and strategies.

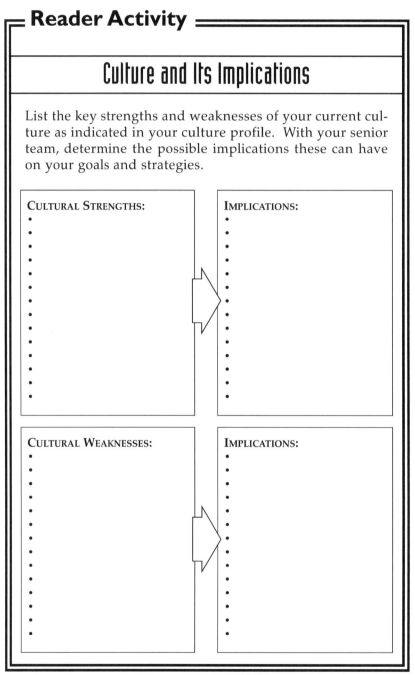

CULTURAL STRENGTHS:
-
-
-
-
-
-
-
-
-
-
-
-
-
-

IMPLICATIONS:
-
-
-
-
-
-
-
-
-
-
-
-
-
-

CULTURAL WEAKNESSES:
-
-
-
-
-
-
-
-
-
-
-
-
-
-

IMPLICATIONS:
-
-
-
-
-
-
-
-
-
-
-
-
-
-

7

PHASE III: BEGIN AT THE TOP

At age 66, Stanley Gault accepted the challenge of turning Goodyear Tire & Rubber around for a reason that was "98% emotional." Because Goodyear is the last major American-owned tire company, Gault was willing to devote three years of his life to rebuilding the company. In an interview with *Fortune Magazine*, he said:

> *We needed a tremendous cultural change involving everyone in the organization. When you're in this kind of jam, time is not on your side.*

One of Gault's first actions was to clarify the future objectives for the company. Using film and television, he transmitted his message worldwide in a way that allowed everyone in the company to see how they fit into the picture — no one was excluded. At the same time, they discontinued using the word "employee"in favor of the term "associate."

After the term "associate" started gaining acceptance, three or four mill workers approached Gault and asked hesitantly if the word "associate" applied to him. Gault was stopped. "Well, I tell you, that really grabbed me, when this guy with 35 years of service...wants to know if the word "associate" applied to me." Gault assured the worker that he was an associate and made a special point to visit the area where he worked. Through the grapevine and e-mail, his actions were transmitted around the world "in 60 seconds," according to Gault.

THE SHADOW OF THE LEADER

A leader doesn't just get the message across—a leader is the message.

—Warren Bennis

What leaders do is as important as what they say. Effective leaders shape the culture of their organizations through a powerful combination of message matched by action. Through their actions, attitudes, and messages, they cast a shadow that influences everyone around them—in the workplace, at home, and in the community.

The shadows of great leaders extend far beyond their own lives. John Fitzgerald Kennedy's actions and messages called for commitment and involvement. Part of his legacy is the Peace Corps and the conquest of space. Mahatma Ghandi and Martin Luther King, Jr. advocated and demonstrated nonviolence, and their nonviolent protests of existing conditions changed the world as we know it.

But, the shadow of the leader is not limited to world leaders. Business leaders, teachers, parents, church and community leaders all cast shadows that influence others. In very meaningful ways, hourly employees who interact with customers are leaders who cast powerful shadows about the company and its real commitment to service. Actions that match the message make the shadow longer, influencing people much more powerfully. Actions that vary from the stated messages or company slogans also demonstrate what's important, and not always in ways that add to the bottom line.

The following organizational charts tell the story of the shadow of the leader:

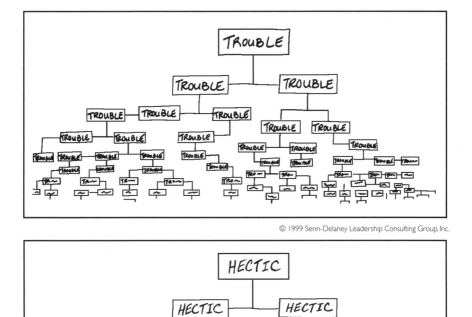

© 1999 Senn-Delaney Leadership Consulting Group, Inc.

Figure 7   © 1999 Senn-Delaney Leadership Consulting Group, Inc.

One of the most intimate and far-reaching examples of this shadow concept happens when parents, perhaps aware of their own imperfections, exhort their children to "Do as I say, not as I do." Unfortunately, children generally tune out that message and mimic the behaviors they see. James Baldwin said:

> *Children have never been very good at listening to their elders, but they have never failed to imitate them.*

The message of any parent or business leader will be drowned out if the actions conflict with the words.

One of our favorite songs from the '60s is good wisdom for parents and corporate executives alike:

Children Learn What They Live

If children live with criticism, they learn to condemn.
If children live with hostility, they learn to fight.
If children live with ridicule, they learn to be shy.
If children live with shame, they learn to feel guilty.
If children live with tolerance, they learn to be patient.
If children live with encouragement, they learn confidence.
If children live with praise, they learn to appreciate.
If children live with fairness, they learn justice.
If children live with security, they learn to have faith.
If children live with approval, they learn to like themselves.
If children live with acceptance and friendship, they learn to
    find love in the world.

—Dorothy Law Nolte

Parenting is a huge responsibility, and too often we forget how our behaviors and attitudes affect our children. Henry Wheeler Shaw once said, *"To bring up a child in the way he should go, travel that way yourself once in a while."*

The role of the leader, at work and at home, requires modeling the desired behavior, letting others see the desired values in action. To become effective leaders, we must become aware of our shadows and then learn to have our actions match our message.

One way to better understand the impact that leadership has upon employees is to make just a little shift in the above poem, then as you read it, picture your organization and your leadership shadow:

Employees Learn From Their Leaders

If employees live with criticism, they learn to blame others.
If employees live with hostility, they learn to resist.
If employees live with ridicule, they learn to avoid risks.
If employees live with shame, they learn to underestimate their
    abilities.
If employees live with tolerance, they learn to learn.

If employees live with encouragement, they learn confidence.
If employees live with praise, they learn to appreciate.
If employees live with fairness, they learn accountability.
If employees live with opportunity, they learn to have faith.
If employees live with approval, they learn to like themselves.
If employees live with acceptance and recognition, they learn to find fulfillment in the workplace.

Warren Deakins, president and CEO of Fidelity Mutual Life Insurance Company, feels strongly about the importance of consistency between actions and words:

I would submit to you that it is unnatural for you to come in late and for your people to come in early. I think it is unnatural for you to be dishonest and your people to be honest. I think it is unnatural for you to not handle your finances well and then to expect your people to handle theirs well. In all these simple things, I think you have to set the standard.

The head of an organization or a team casts a shadow that influences the employees in that group. The shadow may be weak or powerful, but it always exists. It is a reflection of everything the leader does and says. Marjorie M. Blanchard, president of Blanchard Training and Development, Inc., describes it this way:

People are smart. If you say one thing and do another, people see the discrepancies. Every decision I make as a leader in my company is being watched for the meaning and the values behind it. When you make a mistake, you create a negative story that can last a long time. So leaders have to lead by example, and be aware of the impact they create.

Entire corporations often take on aspects of the personality of the senior executive. For instance, Microsoft is known for being innovative and competitive — a direct reflection of Bill Gates— while Wal-Mart's culture of being friendly, thrifty, and customer-focused comes straight from its founder, the late Sam Walton.

Sometimes, corporate cultures are so closely connected to the leader of the organization that it is almost impossible to think of the organization without thinking of the leader as well—Herb Kelleher at Southwest Airlines, John Harvey at ICI, Richard Branson of Virgin Group (Virgin Atlantic Airlines, Virgin Records, etc.), Lee Iacocca at Chrysler, Fred Smith at Federal Express, Walt Disney and the Disney companies. This is the power of the shadow in action; the power to shape and influence the outcome for the organization.

Cultural Implications of the Shadow of the Leader

One of the most common complaints we hear throughout organizations is that the senior team is not walking the talk. Whenever a company begins to make statements about desired behaviors and people don't see those behaviors being modeled at the top, there is a sense of lack of integrity. This can take various forms:

- The organization is asking people to be more open to change, and the top leaders are not changing themselves

- Increased teamwork and cross-organizational collaboration is preached, and the senior team itself is not a good team

- The organization is seen to cut back on expenses, and the senior team doesn't change any of its special perks

- People are being asked to be accountable for results while the senior team members continue to subtly blame one another for lack of results

We have found that the fastest way to create a positive self-fulfilling prophecy about cultural change is to have the leaders individually and collectively shift their own behaviors. They don't have to be perfect, they just have to deal themselves into the same game.

Our years of observing this phenomenon have led us to conclude that culture-shifting initiatives will be successful only if the senior team itself formally engages in a process of changing its own behaviors. When leadership, teambuilding, and culture-shaping trainings are a part of the change process, the senior team should be the first team that takes part. If 360° Feeback Inventory instruments are to be used to measure behaviors, then the senior team should be the first to step up and be measured.

Anyone who has ever worked with training processes with middle management knows his limitations. When attendees are asked about the value of the session, the classic responses are, "My boss is the one who should be attending" or "It sounds great, but that's not the way it is around here, just ask my manager."

Because of the critical need for the senior team to role-model (shadow) the new culture, it is the group that needs to come together in a shared, off-site process to define the guiding behaviors for the organization. Whenever this is delegated to a committee under it or to expert writers, the statements of values may read well, but are not owned by and don't reside in the hearts of the senior team. When the values don't live in the senior team, the probability that the organization will live the values is low.

As a firm that specializes in the area of culture-shaping, we have an unwritten policy that unless we are doing a demonstration or pilot project, we won't design and conduct culture-shaping sessions for clients unless we can first work with the team that leads the organization or a semi-autonomous group. It is not that we would not like the business, it's just that we know that it is unlikely to work.

LEADING CHANGE

Jamie Houghton of Corning Inc. provides an excellent example of how enlightened, dedicated leadership can transform a company. At the time he assumed the CEO position of Corning in 1983, the company was a classic rust-belt organization. Almost 70 percent of the company's business was in mature cyclical markets, and profits had declined for the past three years. In addition, Corning held small-to-modest market shares in its core businesses.

Jamie Houghton brought a focus and sense of urgency to the company. In the same year that he assumed the CEO role, he announced his plan to spend $5 million on the overall objective of "complete customer satisfaction." The company's employees and management were not impressed. Having been through many superficial improvement programs, they believed this was just another "flavor of the month." To combat this, Houghton demonstrated real commitment to the new vision. He appointed the company's first Director of Quality and established a goal of five percent of employees' time devoted to training. He and his corporate management committee were the first graduates of the two-day training course. He established recognition programs such as the Houghton Award, given annually to the division with the most effective customer satisfaction program. He demonstrated his personal commitment by becoming a tireless champion of customer satisfaction throughout the company—meeting with over 50 employee groups yearly. In the words of one employee, "His message has never varied in the past 10 years."

To drive the customer focus down through the organization, he established the "Vital Few." These are the measurements of each division's products and services that are most important to its customers. Each division's performance on its Vital Few measures is tracked regularly by Houghton and the management committee. Progress against these measures is also graphically exhibited throughout the company so that employees are given continual feedback on their performance. The company's reward systems were modified to support the new version with a percent of each employee's salary and bonus being impacted by performance on the Vital Few. In addition, communication and employee opinion are solicited by a number of mechanisms, such as internal customer satisfaction assessments.

All of this activity has transformed the culture of the company. The number of corrective-action suggestions by employees has risen from 800 per year before Houghton assumed leadership to over 16,000 per year. There are now over 2,000 problem-solving teams working on corrective-action programs. These results have also impacted the company's bottom line.

Return on equity, which stood at 7.3% in 1983 was at 14.1% in 1994. Defects at a ceramic production unit were reduced from 10,000 parts per million to 3 parts per million. On-time delivery at its clinical lab testing unit went from 88% to 98.5%. At another unit, customers' deadlines for quotes were missed a full 50% of the time before Houghton's programs were instituted. Now 100% of the quotes are received by the customer on time every time.

Jamie Houghton exhibited vision, commitment, and dedication in his mission to transform the culture at Corning. He has led by example, never letting up over the past 16 years.

BUILDING AN ALIGNED LEADERSHIP TEAM

High-performance, aligned teams do not just happen, even if you have been able to select the best people for the job! Real teams are developed, not assembled, as any basketball or other sports fan can tell you. Having the best talent doesn't mean they will play well together! Achieving the teamwork and alignment necessary to build a high-performance culture is an important task.

Building and maintaining an aligned, high-performance management team is the job of the leader. In many ways, he or she is the team leader, coach, and manager, as well as a player and member of the team. In designing and conducting senior executive team-building sessions for dozens of Fortune 1000 corporations, we have witnessed firsthand the changes that can happen in the culture and performance of an organization by having a real team at the top— one that casts the right shadow.

Senior teams need to come together and devote time to shaping their own team dynamics. All too often, they believe they either don't have the time or they don't see the value in working on themselves versus working on issues. As a result, all too many business meetings are ineffective, unproductive, and too time-consuming. This takes many forms that are all too recognizable:

- Pocket vetoes—people don't confront the decision in the meeting; they just don't follow through on it
- Lack of open dialogue and debate—people don't speak up and the real discussions take place in the halls after the meeting
- Lack of alignment—everyone in the organization knows that different senior team members have conflicting views and directions

- Hidden agendas—major unspoken issues exist that are not surfaced and directly dealt with
- Triangular conversations—team member A talks to B about C, rather than talking directly to C

Teams need to take time to establish team agreements about behaviors or Rules of Engagement. One leader who has used this effectively is David Novak, president of Tricon Global, formerly of the PepsiCo Restaurant group. When he first took over at KFC, he took his team for a three-day off-site to establish team agreements and to create a set of values to define the culture.

One of the agreements they established was "Team Together—Team Apart," which meant many things to them, including:

- We will engage in healthy debate, work to reach alignment on issues, and then all commit to supporting the team's decision, once it's made
- We will represent ourselves as a unified team to the organization
- We will be supportive of one another when we are together and when we are apart
- We will directly address issues with one another, not with third parties; i.e., we will not be critical of each other to others

This and other team agreements helped the team make and execute decisions faster. They were able to focus the energies of all functions on key initiatives and create positive change quickly. This contributed to record results. Much of this was the result of the leadership casting a clear and positive shadow that established the new rules of the road for the entire organization.

8

PHASE IV: DESIGNING A HIGH-PERFORMANCE CULTURE

Make a mental list of distinctive high-performance organizations that are consistently admired by others. We would guess that one or more of the following would come to mind:

- Hewlett Packard
- Wal-Mart
- General Electric
- Federal Express

While they are very different businesses in different markets and with different strategies, what do they have in common? They all have strong and healthy cultures, and they all place a high value on building and maintaining those winning cultures.

The exceptional performance of companies with strong values is documented in Kotter and Heskett's book, *Corporate Culture and Performance*. This important research work followed a number of companies over a ten-year period and concluded:

Organizations that give more than lip service to mission statements, stressing the values of people, are more likely to have effective performance because managers feel energized and willing to help the firm change with the competitive environment.

The values that members of an organization share create a template for corporate and individual behavior. When these values have been clearly stated and accepted by all members of the organization, they set guidelines and standards for making decisions, determining priorities, solving problems, and addressing competitive pressures.

The flip side of a high-performance culture with healthy

shared values is a culture whose values are vague and fragmented and whose culture seems to put up barriers whenever the organization tries to change.

A High-Performance Culture

> *Our job is to provide a culture in which people can flourish and reach their dreams—in which they can be all they want to be.*

—Jack Welch

All cultures are different and there is no one perfect culture just as there is no one perfect personality. While there is no perfect corporate culture, it seems that organizations that possess healthy, high-performance cultures all have a similar feeling about them. In some of our recent senior executive retreats for U.S. corporations, we have been asking people to describe what a high-performance culture would be like. Remarkably, they all tended to come up with a similar feeling and even some of the same words. Many described a high-performance culture this way:

> *It would be a flexible and highly adaptive culture where employees display a "can-do" attitude, a contagious sense of optimism and belief in themselves and their products and services, and where people at all levels feel energized, motivated, and find that they are growing both personally and professionally by being a part of the company. A high-performance culture sees business and people problems as part of the game and tends to keep a healthy perspective and balance between numbers, results, people, and relationships. Everyone has a focus on the customer, knows what is important, where the company is going, and can't wait to beat the pants off the competition.*

One manager in a recent workshop described it this way:

> *There's a lightness here that makes working long hours seem energizing instead of stressful and tiresome!*

Sound ideal?
Sound impossible?
Worth having?

High-performance organizations do exist, but they don't happen by accident, nor without visionary and committed leadership. During our research for the book, *21st Century Leadership*, the kinds of winning shared values the leaders mentioned repeatedly included:

- Integrity and honesty
- Empowering leadership
- Openness and trust
- Teamwork and mutual support
- Caring
- Openness to change
- Quality, service, and a customer focus
- Respect for the individual and for diversity
- Winning and being the best
- Innovation
- Personal accountability
- A can-do attitude
- Balance in life
- Positive and optimistic
- Customer focused

As a result of our work, we have also compiled a list of distinctions between our cultural barriers and winning behaviors.

Cultural Barriers versus Winning Behaviors

Cultural Barriers	Winning Behaviors
• Hierarchical leadership — boss driven	• Empowering leadership
• Turf issues	• Teamwork and mutual support
• Opportunism and lack of principles	• Ethics and integrity
• Hidden agendas, dishonesty, and lack of openness	• Open, honest, and flowing communication
• Distrust and fear	• Trust
• Short-term and strictly bottom-line driven	• Long-term quality, service, and excellence
• Task-oriented and internally focused	• Customer/market-oriented and externally focused
• "Can't be done" attitude	• "Can do" spirit
• Blame and making excuses	• Personal responsibility and accountability
• Co-dependence and excessive independence	• Interdependence
• Prejudiced and judgmental	• Embracing diversity and differences
• Insufficient training	• Continuous learning and knowledge development
• Stress and burnout	• Focus and balance
• Holding onto the past and resisting change	• Innovation, ingenuity, and breakthroughs
• Strict rules and rigid policies	• Flexible, fluid, and rapidly responsive
• Win/Lose games	• Win/Win games and bigger wins for entire organization
• Command and control	• Coaching—appreciative and constructive feedback

CORE VALUES IN HIGH-PERFORMANCE CULTURES

While companies have distinct cultures, we have found that there is an amazing similarity of core values in successful organizations. It's almost as if there is a set of principles of organizational effectiveness that is akin to principles of life effectiveness for people. While they are stated in different ways, combined in different ways, and prioritized in different ways, the list in one form or another includes the following elements:

- Integrity
- Openness and Trust
- Respect for the Individual
- Personal Accountability and Empowerment
- Openness to Change and Innovation
- Feedback and Coaching
- Teamwork
- Organizational Health

These are often personalized or emphasized in different ways. Welch talks about "unyielding integrity," a "boundary-less organization," and "relishing change." The leader of a pharmaceutical organization that depends upon new, innovative products uses the word "trailblazing" to represent innovation and change. An insurance client, Mutual of Omaha, substitutes the phrase "solution seekers" for accountability, and the CEO of a savings and loan uses "relentless drive for improvement."

FOUNDATION VALUES

The purpose of values is to provide a road map for behaviors in the organization. Three of the values are what might be called foundation values (Figure 8.1). While by themselves they don't ensure results, without them an organization is crippled. Those are:

- Ethics and Integrity
  - Mutual Respect
    - Openness and Trust

Any great edifice will last only as long as the foundation that supports it. Similarly, high-performance cultures must be built upon a solid foundation of ethics and integrity, mutual respect, and openness and trust. Without these three foundation principles firmly in place in the hearts, minds, and policies of the leaders and employees, attempts to create a new culture that will draw out all the creative energies and ideas of its people will be wasted.

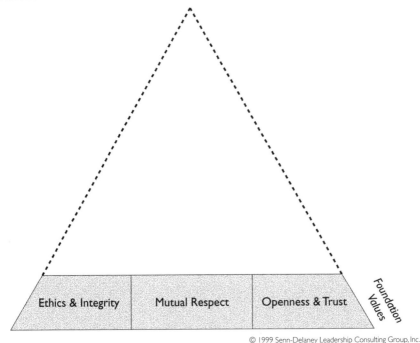

Figure 8.1

- ETHICS AND INTEGRITY

Integrity is not a 90 percent thing, not a 95 percent thing: Either you have it or you don't.

—Peter Scotese, retired CEO, Spring Industries

Ethics and integrity are a cornerstone of all high-performance cultures. The word "integrity" implies consistency or congruence between words and deeds, while "ethics" suggests a system of moral standards that an organization or individual uses to guide decisions and daily behaviors. The most common elements of ethics and integrity are honesty, fairness, compassion, and social responsibility.

We have found that most leaders, when talking about values, emphasize ethics and integrity as a foundation value. Unless the bedrock of a leader's life, or an organization, or a government is built on integrity, instability will ensue. As David Kearns, former chairman and CEO of Xerox Corporation, said, "It's absolutely imperative that we have a cadre of people coming up into the leadership core that really understands the issue of integrity."

While virtually all businesses speak highly of the need for integrity and pride themselves on being models of modern business integrity, a deeper examination of the meaning of the word reveals that today's definitions are somewhat lacking. Integrity draws from the same root as the word "integer."

A person of high integrity is not only honest, he or she also sends a single and singular message of being one person and of one mind on an issue. This is manifested in many ways, including not communicating different messages to different audiences, not talking out of both sides of one's mouth, practicing what one preaches, walking the talk, and getting the hips to move in the same direction as the lips. Texans traditionally refer to integrity with a clarity that draws from their heritage: "Don't write a check with your mouth that your body can't cash!"

Leaders involved in major business change activities soon learn that not honoring verbal commitments is a failing in "integrity" in the eyes of employees. This awareness, when combined with the pressures of business change, can have profound impact on how a change initiative is presented and managed. Speeches and communications with employees take on a new sense of seriousness in an effort not to violate their integrity, like hedging on the job elimination questions, since it quickly weakens the foundation of the entire process.

Leadership by example is an imperative for high-performance cultures. Leaders must demonstrate consistency between message and behavior — they must walk their talk. High-performance cultures generally develop a code of ethics that clearly spells out behavioral expectations for the organization and its members. This code is used as the basis for spreading an increased level of candor throughout the culture so that honesty and fairness become the normal way of interacting. This code creates a clear sense of right and wrong and establishes a line that is not to be crossed. That doesn't mean that the organization isn't aggressive or competitive, but it does mean that the organization's actions are consistent with its values. John D. Macomber, while chairman and president of Export-Import Bank of the United States, put it this way: "Great companies have always walked on a high ethical, moral plane." While this may run counter to the conventional wisdom held by the public at large, employees of these great companies generally feel that they operate from a strong ethical base.

• MUTUAL RESPECT

> *You build a team when you consider the well-being of each person on your team.*
>
> —Sanford "Sandy" McDonnell, Chairman Emeritus
> of McDonnell Douglas Corporation

In today's business environment, employees differ in gender, race, ethnic background, and age. Being able to deal with the many issues of diversity is fundamental to organizational performance. Many experts on diversity and its impact on organizational performance strongly believe that unless mutual respect is firmly embedded in the corporate culture, diversity training and other programs will fail to make positive inroads.

Mutual respect in organizations is easier to see than to define. Its essence lies in the way we treat others and the way we design our policies and organizational systems. The elements of mutual respect include human resource fundamentals such as pay and benefits, but go well beyond them to reflect a recognition of the importance of every individual to the organization. It includes pleasant, functional working spaces, open access to other members of the organization regardless of rank or position, a sharing of information and rewards, a high level of training and development, and involvement in the planning of work processes.

Mutual respect is often reflected in terms such as "associates" or "partners" instead of workers or employees. Mutual respect assumes that each person in the organization is capable and well-meaning. Rather than trying to control individual actions, the high-performance culture concentrates on creating an environment where people can function at their highest levels.

• OPENNESS AND TRUST

Trust is the key value of our times.

—James E. Burke, former Chairman
of Johnson & Johnson

When employees believe that the organization and its leaders are ethical and have integrity, and there is an atmosphere of mutual respect, it is possible to create an environment of openness and trust. This environment is open to new ideas, honest communication, and different points of view. It promotes feedback—both appreciative and constructive—which facilitates problem identification and solution. Conversely, environments that do not have open, honest communication tend to preclude new ideas and change because of the possibility of failure and therefore, criticism.

John Allison, chairman of BB&T Financial, an outstanding performing regional bank based in North Carolina, has led the transformation of his organization from a laggard to a star, using a fierce belief in people, purpose, and trust:

You have to be serious about trust. Most businesses do not trust their employees. Trust is a personal thing. I literally trust everyone that works for me. They are not perfect, but that is different. If you do not trust them, chances are, they do not trust you.

In an open and trusting environment, employees at all levels are encouraged to "tell it like it is," challenge old ways of doing things, bring up new ideas, and focus on solutions and possibilities. This type of candid and open environment can only occur when people have trust and are able to separate the person from their behavior or actions.

Performance Values

While values like integrity, trust and respect provide a sound foundation for an organization, they do not ensure success. What is it that separates the winners from the losers? It is not only the skills, competencies, and foundation values, but a specific mind-set of individuals and teams that makes the difference. The critical performance values we've identified include:

- Teamwork
- Personal Accountability and Empowerment
- Flexibility (Openness to Change)
- A Commitment to Continuous Learning and Personal Growth through Coaching

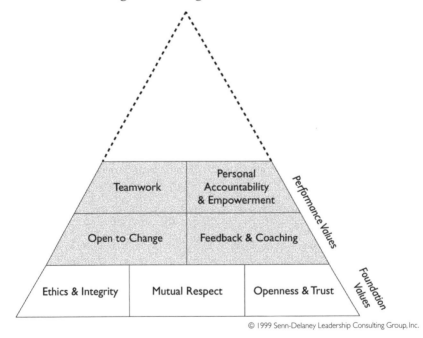

© 1999 Senn-Delaney Leadership Consulting Group, Inc.

Figure 8.2

• TEAMWORK

When teamwork kicks in, nobody can beat you.

—Don Shula, head coach, Miami Dolphins
(the only NFL team to attain a perfect 17–0 season)

Today's complex business environment requires interdependence of individuals and departments. Implementing changes and serving customers requires people to work together in ways not required previously. In a high-performance culture, teamwork replaces individualism and competition between departments. The essence of teamwork is the belief and understanding that all people in the organization belong to the same team and must work together to achieve the overall goals. It's the understanding that, "I don't succeed unless and until the entire team succeeds."

An effective team is a group of people acting together in an atmosphere of trust and accountability who agree that the best way to achieve a common goal is to cooperate!

The ability to develop and lead good teams is the number one leadership skill required in today's organizations. Downsizing, right-sizing, reorganizing, and reengineering are all indications of the pressure on organizations to reduce the costs of doing business in today's highly competitive environment. This often leaves departments and work groups with the same (or more) work to do with fewer people. Teamwork is not just nice to have, it is a requirement for success.

Total Quality Improvement, superior customer service, and other forms of improving competitiveness are all based on good teamwork principles. Without teamwork, these improvement efforts generally end in frustration and even alienation.

The lack of teamwork can be extremely expensive. We have seen competing internal groups spend millions of dollars of their own and their external consultant's time trying to prove another division or function wrong. This extreme competitiveness often results in the withholding of critical information from a competing group, regardless of the damage to the entire organization.

Jon Katzenbach of McKinsey & Company and co-author of *The Wisdom of Teams*, speaks about teamwork with real passion. When asked why team training is so popular, he replies: "Because teams produce extra performance results. There is virtually no environment in which teams—if done right—can't have a measurable impact on the performance of an organization."

While these benefits are critical to the success of an organization, there is also a set of softer benefits of teamwork that greatly enhance the working environment:

- Teamwork fills the real human need for socialization
- People learn from each other in a team environment
- Working together for a common goal is both motivating and provides a real sense of purpose and fulfillment

- ACCOUNTABILITY AND EMPOWERMENT

For the last two decades, the most exercised part of the corporate body has been the pointed finger!

—Tom Peters

Many of our culture-change clients consider "accountability" the *make it happen* ingredient!

When individuals understand personal accountability and that their actions enable them to positively influence almost any situation, they become a key ingredient in the high-performance organization.

"Don't Blame Me!" How many times have you heard that statement uttered in anguish inside an organization? In the book, *A Nation of Victims*, author Charles J. Sykes points to the decline in American competitiveness and the erosion in our quality of life as being linked to a general feeling of lack of control; a sense of having no power over events or circumstances. Sykes refers to this as "the victimization of America." He references a series of magazine articles that highlight this sense of victimization:

- *New York Magazine*—"The New Culture of Victimization: Don't Blame Me!"
- *Time*—"Crybabies: Eternal Victims"
- *Esquire*—"A Confederacy of Complainers"
- *Harpers*—"Victims All?"

Victim attitudes abound in organizations: blaming, excuses, "CYA" activities, "it's not my job," "they did it," and hundreds of other behaviors and attitudes that people use as a shield against taking risks and accepting their own personal accountability. These negative attitudes directly impact productivity, efficiency, and the bottom line.

Accountable attitudes are also present in organizations. Without them, nothing would ever get accomplished. Some teams and organizations overcome enormous obstacles with their tremendous sense of personal and organizational accountability.

Accountability is the belief that an individual's actions or inactions are the major determinant of success or lack of success. Accountable people believe that they have a great deal of control over their own destiny, and use their ability to make choices as their greatest tool to influence outcomes and create results.

Choice, not chance, determines destiny.

People can enhance their personal reponsibility, while shedding non-productive victim attitudes, by increasing their awareness of accountability and recognizing their ability to choose the attitudes that are most productive for them.

People with personal accountability tend to look for the best points present in every situation. They know that by being aware of all the clues, they can determine the best choices that will most positively influence the outcome. When a situation doesn't go well, they ask themselves a lot of questions about why things didn't turn out the way they expected. And, they look first at their own actions, asking such questions as the following:

- What clues didn't I see?
- What extra steps could I have taken?
- What actions did I avoid?

- What should I have known?
- Who should I have confronted sooner?
- What personality traits or habits of mine might have aggravated this situation?

While it is true that the higher the level of personal accountability, the better the overall outcome of a situation, it is not humanly possible to be 100 percent accountable all of the time. Expecting that kind of accountability from yourself or employees is not realistic and often creates a great deal of negative pressure in which results start to dramatically suffer.

Where do accountable individuals draw the line when there is almost always more that could be done? The answer to this seemingly endless pursuit of perfection lies in the Serenity Prayer attributed to American theologian Reinhold Niebuhr:

Grant me the serenity to accept the things I cannot change, the courage to change the things I can, and the wisdom to know the difference.

An underlying theme of every performance-improvement approach is the involvement and development of people — or "empowerment." An environment that fosters the growth and involvement of all employees creates the raw material needed to produce greater productivity, process improvement, and innovation. Empowerment means that people are more involved in the design of their work and in the decisions that affect them. As a result, they feel more ownership in the process and more committed to achieving the objectives.

Bill Gates, CEO of Microsoft, has led one of the world's most remarkable high-growth companies of this century. He describes empowerment as a necessary skill of leadership:

As we look ahead into the next century, leaders will be those who empower others.... Empowering leadership means bringing out the energy and capabilities that people have and getting them to work together in a way they wouldn't do otherwise. That requires that they see the positive impact they can have and sense the opportunities.

The kind of empowerment that creates exceptional results is made up of two major elements: the letting go of tight controls by leadership and the acceptance of personal accountability by all employees.

The foundation of empowerment is an understanding that by getting people involved in all aspects of their work, they will perform better in the long run and be more committed to the organization. In a culture of empowerment, the organization's systems, policies, and management behaviors encourage decisions by individuals and teams.

However, empowerment, employee involvement, or participative management alone, without additional elements of responsibility, trust, and respect, will not be effective. Before empowerment can be effective, individuals must have a mind-set of personal accountability. In a high-performance organization of accountability and empowerment, the work environment seems turbocharged.

A common error often made is in the area of empowerment. While there's no question that a healthy culture promotes empowerment, companies can't mandate empowerment. In fact, when organizations make broad statements about empowering their people, it often backfires. When people who feel victimized by downsizing and change are told that they are going to be empowered, it provides fertile ground for added victim statements. "I'm not empowered, you won't give me the budget." "I'm not empowered, you didn't let me make that change." While empowerment is an important value, it is often best not to state it explicitly. Instead the focus should be on personal accountability and a can-do attitude, which is self-empowerment.

Empowered people believe that they make significant changes in the world around them. When you have that philosophy, there's nothing that can't be done.

—Barbara Levy Kipper, chairman of Chas. Levy Company

• FLEXIBILITY (OPENNESS TO CHANGE)

Whenever you face a steepening slope of change, that is the time when you especially need wise leadership.

—Bernadine Healy, director of National Institutes of Health

Never before have organizations been required to shift so dramatically to encompass such a variety of capabilities and talents in order to succeed. Organizational agility has become an imperative. Today, we can't plan years ahead. Instead, we need to be agile enough to respond to changing markets and to capture opportunities. A key challenge now facing all leaders is how to effectively master the art of change. Change is not easy, especially with the habits built up from our previous paradigms of leadership.

Change comes in many dimensions. It includes a personal willingness to be open to continuous self-examination and introspection. One large corporation we studied was headed by a leader who talked almost exclusively about the past—the good old days. In this and other ways he signaled that he had stopped growing, and the organization was feeling the effects. People who embrace change recognize that reaching one's potential as a leader or a person is a journey—not a destination.

Another dimension of change is a person's ability to be an effective change agent by learning to introduce change and lead it. In today's fast-moving business world, a change agent is someone who invites and fuels innovation and looks for ways to improve everything. A third dimension is seeing possibilities in new ideas. One of the traditional beliefs about being a leader is, "If I'm shown a new idea, my job is to figure out what's wrong with it." This is what we learned and practiced in "management-by-exception." We are taught to be an "observer-critic;" someone who challenges new ideas, plays devil's advocate, and tries to find inconsistencies. In this new era of change, it is important that cultures and people develop a flexibility that embraces change. Jack Welch used the words "relish change" as a part of GE's Leaders' Values.

• FEEDBACK AND COACHING

> *Personally, I'm always ready to learn, though I do not always like being taught.*

> —Winston Churchill

In this time of change, the world demands a continuous level of improvement: shorter lead times, increased productivity, new skills, new products, new services, better communication, ever higher levels of mastery. For companies to be effective in this rapidly changing environment, their leaders need to understand what motivates the people around them, as well as themselves.

For years the theory of motivation revolved around the carrot and the stick. Managers were taught that motivating people was a matter of rewarding them for good actions and punishing them for bad actions. In organizations that use this theory, people spend most of their time avoiding the stick.

We now know that human motivation is much more complex than the simplistic idea of the carrot and stick; people respond to a variety of things. The following list was prepared by Rick Maurer in his book, *Caught in the Middle:*

- **Meaning**—people want to know that what they are doing is important to the company or organization they work for. They also want to know that somehow, no matter how remote the connection, they are "making the world a better place." They want to "make a difference."

- **Results**—people like to see the results of their efforts. There's a sense of accomplishment and fulfillment that comes from successfully completing a task. Seeing the results of their efforts gives people a way to measure their progress.

- **Challenge**—people want to learn and grow. They progress by doing new things that make them stretch and develop new skills and capabilities.

- **Respect and Recognition**—people want acknowledgment for the things they do well. Recognition can be as simple as a pat on the back or as elaborate as a formal awards ceremony. An environment of respect and dignity gives everyone a foundation for giving their best efforts.

- **Control**—People want to have some say in the decision-making process. They want to be involved in what happens to them and around them; they want to feel empowered.

While motivation differs from person to person, this list is probably consistent with what most people want and, also, basically describes a coaching environment. This atmosphere creates the conditions necessary for people to do their best and feel good about what they are doing. The important characteristics of the coaching environment include:

- A caring and supportive climate
- A coaching mentality among leaders
- Constructive feedback requested and given freely at all levels
- A balance of appreciation and constructive input

Appreciation is probably the simplest and least-expensive method of motivating and rewarding people. Saying thanks, putting Post-it notes on paychecks, posting complimentary letters from customers, and celebrating outstanding efforts are simple, inexpensive ways to let people know they are appreciated and valued.

Just as important as expressing appreciation for work well

done is providing constructive feedback on how to improve performance. All employees want to know how to do their jobs better. Studies show that most employees feel they do not receive enough coaching and feedback. Because they don't know how they're doing, they don't know what to change in order to improve.

A high-performance organization is one in which individuals encourage each other to expand their knowledge, increase their productivity, and reach their potential. Employees see one important part of their job descriptions as "coach." The coach helps people become winners who reach their peak performance. A healthy, growth-oriented work environment is one that is feedback rich. It provides the information people need to continuously improve their performance.

Adding Meaning to Core Values: Defining Guiding Behaviors

A professed value such as teamwork is not specific enough to guide and align people's behaviors. To some it might mean being a good team player in their department, to others it might mean being a team contributor to the broader organization. Personal accountability to one person might mean doing my own job well and no more, while to others it might mean looking for any ways they can contribute to the overall success of the organization.

We've been asked on many occasions to look at why culture-shaping initiatives are not working, even though a company may have written values. What we find is that there are a wide variety of interpretations of what those values mean. We have concluded that it's critical in the culture-shaping process to very explicitly define each core value with a set of guiding behaviors that clearly defines the behaviors appropriate for that value.

An example of the way we define teamwork at Senn-Delaney Leadership via guiding behaviors is shown below:

TEAMWORK—GUIDING BEHAVIORS

1. Acts for the long-term benefit of the company even when it may take away from short-term personal benefits.
2. Develops positive working relationships with peers and others.
3. Supports fellow teammates to succeed.
4. Involves others in discussing issues and resolving conflicts.
5. Acknowledges others who demonstrate teamwork.
6. Informs and involves teammates whenever possible.
7. Seeks win/win solutions.
8. Shares information and resources with others.
9. Credits others for their contributions.

© 1999 Senn-Delaney Leadership Consulting Group, Inc.

As you can see, teamwork goes beyond being willing to cooperate. In this definition it requires someone to not be territorial, but, in fact, be willing to sacrifice individual or departmental goals in order to accomplish a bigger win for the overall organization.

Guiding behaviors also allow a company to much more specifically define the unique differences and the priorities in their own culture. They also provide some flexibility in terms of how many categories of values are needed since, for example, respect for individuals could be a guiding behavior under teamwork, and creative thinking or innovation could be a guiding behavior under embracing change.

Guiding behaviors provide one more critical aspect for the organization; they furnish a very specific list of observable behaviors that can become the foundation of a human resources' reinforcement system. This system might include performance appraisals, 360° Feedback Inventory Reports, and hiring and firing criteria.

VISION: THE DIRECTIONAL PRINCIPLE FOR PURPOSE AND MEANING

While values and guiding behaviors can describe how people operate within an organization, more is needed to provide the fire and energy needed for today's corporations to compete in the highly competitive global marketplace. That energizing factor is Vision.

> *Vision is extremely valuable for rallying the spirit, feeling, and commitment of our people.*
>
> —John Pepper, president of The Procter & Gamble Company

At the very top of the high-performance pyramid is Vision (Figure 8.3). It is the capstone that brings the organization together, without which it is an incomplete structure without purpose.

> *Where there is no vision, the people will perish.*
>
> —Proverbs 29:18

We use the metaphor of the operation of a bicycle. The rear wheel, like the culture, provides the power for forward movement. The front wheel, like vision, mission, and strategy, directs the bicycle along the right path.

High-performance organizations combine a compelling vision of the future, a clear set of strategies, and a high-performance culture.

Vision is the magnetic force that unleashes the drive, energy, creativity, and courage needed to reach an objective. Compelling visions have empowered and released human and organizational potential throughout history. The powerful vision of a land where people were equal and able to control their own destinies allowed the fledgling American colony to wrest freedom from the much larger, better-financed British crown.

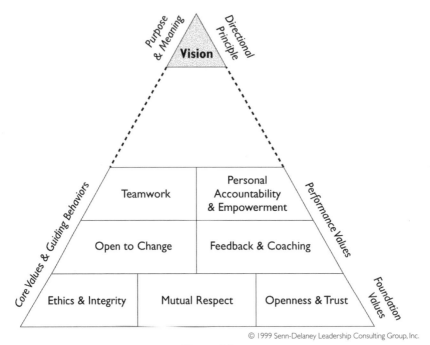

Figure 8.3

The vision of a man on the moon set into motion an enormous effort combining government, industry, and educational institutions. It changed our perception of the universe forever. The vision of change driven by a computer that could be used by anyone and everyone led a small group of Apple Computer employees to develop the Macintosh—a computer that set a new standard for ease of use and accessibility.

In human endeavors, thought precedes action. We have to know where we're going in order to get there. The more clearly we can see the final destination and the more we want to be there, the more energy we will have to overcome any obstacles in our path. A compelling vision consists of two elements: a future-state that captures our imagination and a passionate desire to reach it.

Vision is a primary ingredient of success, whether by an individual, a team, a company, or a country. It's impossible to wake up one morning and say, "I'm going to be a success" and have it happen. You need to be a success at something. Only when the vision is clearly defined, does the path to success reveal itself.

In many ways, a clear vision represents "magnetic north" for employees within a high-performance organization. It represents the idealized picture of what the company and its employees can become. A vision is much more than just an objective or picture of a future; it evokes strong feelings. It is the feeling, not the objective, that tends to inspire employees with high energy and commitment.

Vision imparts a clear picture of who we are, where we are going, and why it is important to us. Vision appeals to the more noble, cause-oriented elements within all human beings and, as such, unleashes creative energies and uplifts the spirits of employees throughout the organization. Vision transforms strategies and missions into a way of life and significantly narrows the gap between plans on paper and forceful actions in the competitive marketplace.

Many companies make the common mistake of equating a mission statement and a vision. In a sense, they believe that goal setting and strategic planning are the same as envisioning. While mission and strategy spell out the "how to"s in a company's quest for competitive advantage, vision is the "why to"s that motivate people to give their best with enthusiasm and commitment. People do not spring out of bed in the morning shouting, "Oh boy, another day of earnings per share," but they arise early and stay late to fulfill their vision.

Just as President Kennedy used the vision of a "man on the moon within the decade" to unleash the creativity of the nation to conquer the obstacles of manned space flight, so numerous businesses, even whole industries, have been built by the inspiring power of a vision.

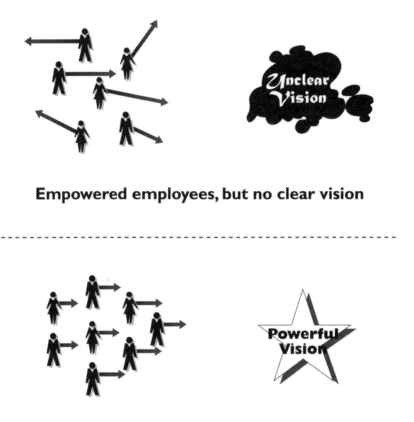

Empowered employees, but no clear vision

Empowered employees; clear, powerful vision

Figure 8.4

The automobile industry, virtually non-existent at the beginning of the 20th century, was pulled into being by the vision of Henry Ford to "provide safe, reliable transportation for the common man!" The modern telecommunications industry, which touches every part of our business and personal lives, gathered strength from the vision of Theodore Vail for a phone in every home and a commitment to "universal service, end to end." The photography industry is now a worldwide, multibillion dollar business, but its founding organization, the Eastman Kodak Company, "began with the vision of one man who saw a way to meet a very special need: The need to picture, share, and preserve the times, people, places, and events of our lives!"

In our work, we have found a number of universal themes that resonate with most people because they touch a core deep inside them. The first is a vision that improves the quality of life. For example, Bill Gates, of Microsoft, stated that his vision is "to put a PC on everyone's desk." This vision, when achieved, will make people more effective and improve their lives. A second universal vision is to serve people in some way; for example, by having the best service or providing exceptional value. The third is to be a part of an excellent, winning team. People will mobilize around a vision that calls for being the best at what they do. A well-stated vision for an organization plays the same role as purpose does for an individual: Both are motivational and directional.

Our own vision has guided the growth and development of the Senn-Delaney Leadership Consulting Group for the past 20 years:

Making a Difference Through Leadership ™

We are a healthy, high-performance team, making a difference in the lives of people, the effectiveness of teams, and the spirit and performance of organizations!

Principles for Alignment

While an energizing vision and a set of core values and guiding behaviors define the subjective elements of business success, a healthy culture with unclear strategies and a poor competitive focus is a design to fail in today's fast-paced, global marketplace. Now that we have a high-performance culture, what do we focus it on? A vision is compelling and energizing, but not specific enough to determine capital allocations or budgets. A clear business mission and goals are needed (Figure 8.5).

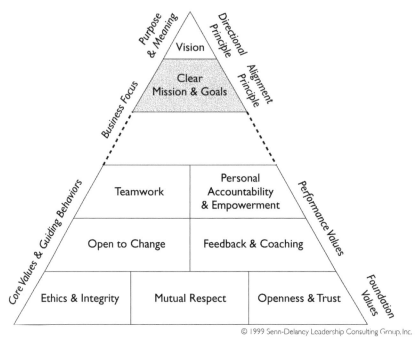

© 1999 Senn-Delaney Leadership Consulting Group, Inc.

Figure 8.5

• CLEAR MISSION AND GOALS

If you don't know where you are going, every road will get you nowhere!

—Henry Kissinger

People want and need a clear path to follow. They need to know where the organization is going and what they're trying to accomplish. Without a clear mission and goals, every person in the organization is determining their own path. Some organizations follow a cow path through the woods, but high-performance organizations are aligned and speed along a superhighway that is clearly defined.

Effective organizations communicate the mission and goals to everyone in the organization so that everyone's going in the same direction, working for the same objectives.

General Electric Power Generation is a highly focused organization that is achieving excellent financial results in a rapidly changing industry whose changes and increased competitive pressures have made it difficult for many organizations to survive. One of the reasons for the success of GE Power Generation is its focus on a clear mission and goals.

Our Mission	Be Recognized as the World's Leader in the Supply of Power Generation Equipment, Services, and Systems
Our Commitments	Provide Our Customers with Products and Services of Such Excellence that GEPG is their Natural Choice
	Create an Environment Where all Employees Can Make a Difference and Grow to Their Full Potential
	Provide an Attractive Return to Our GE Shareholders on their Investments in our Business
	Behave as a Socially Responsible Member of the Communities in Which We Operate

Key Business Objectives

- Set the Industry Standard of Excellence for Customer Satisfaction
- Achieve Total Quality
- Maintain Clear Technology Leadership
- Market Share Leadership through a Market-Back Focus on Customer Needs
- Meet Business and Financial Commitments

These goals and the mission are so important to the company that all employees have pocket cards with the mission and goals printed on them that they carry with them throughout their daily activities at work. The pocket cards serve as a reminder of the importance of the mission and are also used in meetings as a reference for day-to-day decision-making.

PRINCIPLES FOR COMPETITIVE SUCCESS

Quality and customer service are our greatest competitive advantage for the next century.

—Kenneth Chenault, American Express

Having a culture that supports people and creates empowered teams with good coaching and feedback skills is important, but not sufficient for success in today's competitive marketplace. The best internal working environment, with a misdirected business strategy, is an invitation to disaster.

© 1999 Senn-Delaney Leadership Consulting Group, Inc.

Figure 8.6

Most organizations now realize that quality and customer service are the two most effective long-term strategies for doing business in today's competitive, rapidly changing new economy. "Meeting or exceeding customer expectations" is common language in high-performance organizations.

There are two strategic principles that typify all high-performance organizations: an unending focus on customer satisfaction and an obsessive concern for quality. Success in the marketplace requires adherence to these principles (Figure 8.6).

- Customer Focus
- Quality

One of the understandable debates that goes on with most teams working on culture is "Where does our focus on the customer and on quality fit? Is customer focus one of our values, or do we incorporate it in our vision and mission?" As with most debates in the subjective realm, there is no right answer. Some companies focus their vision on the customer, and then the values and the guiding behaviors define how they are going to achieve that. Others highlight customer focus as a key value of the organization, while for some, because of its importance, it's included in both places. However it is handled, it is a key part of the overall model of a high-performance organization.

• CUSTOMER FOCUS

The purpose of a business is to create and keep a customer.

—Theodore Levitt, *The Marketing Imagination*

Everything else aside, there's only one player in the game of business who holds the money — the customer. And customers vote with their dollars. Businesses are voted in or out of existence by their ability to create value for the customer—something the customer will trade dollars for.

High-performance companies listen to their customers extensively. Market research is a constant, broad-based activity, not just the domain of one department. In high-performance companies, customers are a real presence to everyone in the organization: customers are pictured with the product, letters from customers are posted, front-line workers visit customer sites, and customer-focus groups are conducted throughout the organization. The organization continuously talks about what the customer wants, when they want it, and how much they will pay for it.

In the Corning Employee Handbook on Quality, Jamie Houghton, CEO, has put his thoughts down about how important a customer focus is for the survival of the company. The following is an excerpt from this material:

CUSTOMERS: WHO'S ON FIRST?

*In the not-too-distant past most corporations treated customers as an
annoyance at best. The only service customers could count on was
"lip." Today's customers aren't passive recipients of goods and services. They want quality products and services, and they give their
business accordingly. They come to the table with expectations and
requirements.*

*At Corning, customers are valued partners in the business. We're
focusing the company on customer results by providing our employees with the tools to help them measure and meet those customer
expectations. We're also providing special support for our own front-
line soldiers: the customer service representatives.*

*All in all, it's turning the traditional organizational pyramid on its
ear. And that's just fine with us.*

• QUALITY

*Regardless of the exact definition, quality and satisfaction are
determined ultimately by the customer's perception of a total product's value or service relative to its competition.*

—Ronald M. Fortuna, Ernst & Young

Quality balances customer service with cost. It's an equation that
constantly fluctuates as competing companies become more effective at meeting the needs of their customers. One competitor
announces a new model or category of service and the equation
shifts. Another competitor lowers prices, and, again, the balance
shifts. Still another competitor improves quality and the perception
of value changes. High-performance companies are constantly
striving to maximize the value equation by improving quality,
reducing cost, and giving better service.

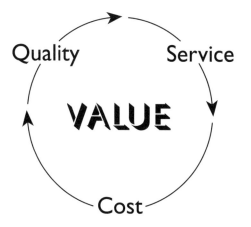

The story of how Xerox won the Malcolm Baldrige Quality Award really began in 1982 when Xerox was on the verge of going out of business. Under the leadership of David Kearns, the top 25 senior officers signed up for creating a high-performance culture founded on quality. The first decision to be made was "What is Quality?" In a week-long off-site workshop, they defined quality as "meeting customer requirements." That meant knowing what those requirements were and meeting them 100 percent of the time.

By turning Xerox into a fierce competitor in the copier, document creation, and transmission marketplace, reviving the fortunes of the company, and winning the Malcolm Baldrige Award, Kearns and his senior management team went beyond the short-term objective of quarterly returns. They put into place a key strategic principle in creating a high-performance culture that will deliver high levels of shareholder returns for years to come.

Moving Vision and Values into the 21st Century

This high-performance model of vision, mission, and values will vary for each organization, but the basics are universal.

© 1999 Senn-Delaney Leadership Consulting Group, Inc.

Figure 8.7

Much of the power comes from the efforts of the senior team in aligning around their set of guiding behaviors or values. New learnings can also lead to shifts in the value set. This has been the case at Senn-Delaney Leadership where, after more than a decade operating with our values, we've added a new dimension: operating from a healthy state of mind. It is the most powerful change we could have made because when realized, it will allow us—individually and collectively—to create more results, and at the same time, live more balanced and fulfilling lives at work and at home. This new dimension is described in the next chapter.

9

GETTING MORE RESULTS AND FULFILLMENT IN LIFE

Principles for Organizational Health

In our work with organizations and executives, we hear more about stress than ever before. As one executive put it, "I can't seem to keep up, and I'm not being very effective. My family sees me less, I've given up exercise and still don't have enough time."

With downsizing, increased competition, and too many change initiatives, most managers are working more hours than ever before. For too many people, balance in life has been lost, and the quality of relationships with spouses and children has suffered.

Stress is taking a toll on the physical "health" of organizations and individuals. Stress often shows up not only physically, but in the state of mind (moods) of individuals.

Our recent work on further strengthening the culture of our own firm has led us to conclude that there is a sub-foundation to high-performance cultures. This deeper foundation is based upon principles for organizational health and includes the state of mind or moods of individuals and the organization, plus the ability of people to be present in the moment, rather than distracted by thoughts of the past or the future. Gaining an understanding of this phenomenon is the key to more balance and fulfillment.

The benefits are enormous. A frenzied and stressed state of mind tends to decrease our effectiveness. The book *Emotional Intelligence: Why It Can Matter More Than IQ* by Daniel P. Goleman makes an excellent case that we lose our wisdom and have, in effect, lower IQ when we are in a lower mood state. This can be seen in the unhealthy bunker mentality that exists in many companies going through change. As one executive put it, "We are reducing head count by 8%, but people are acting as if, just this year, we are cutting 98%." In extreme cases, partial paralysis can take place. More time is spent on rumors, speculation, and avoiding change than on running the business.

Since our thoughts create our perceived reality, it is the nature of our thoughts and our thinking that determines our state of mind and moods. Stress is not caused by downsizing, mergers, or change. Stress is a result of negative thinking *about* downsizing, mergers, or change. The empowering part of this new realization is that while we can't control the fact that the business world is changing, we can influence our thinking.

STATES OF MIND—MOODS & BE HERE NOW

• MOODS

Have you ever tried to give or receive coaching and feedback with a loved one or an employee when you were irritated, angry, or generally in a bad mood? How well did that work? Chances are, not as well as if you had been in a more positive frame of mind.

We can be better team players, better coaches, be more accountable, more open, and accept change better when we are in higher states of mind. Our state of mind often takes the form of moods (see Figure 9.1), which move from high to low, much like an elevator. While they are a part of the normal human condition, our moods have great implications. Some people not only ride the mood elevator, but get off and seem to fully furnish the lower floors, including defensiveness, blame, and judgment. At a business meeting, a group tries to explore issues or make decisions while at the lower mood levels, and wonders why their meetings are so draining and few conclusions are reached.

An important question is what is, normal in the organization? Are fear, frustration, mistrust, unhealthy conflict, and high stress a way of life? Even unhealthy states can become normal to us and therefore become invisible. It's like living alongside a freeway for a few months and no longer noticing the noise or the fumes. We can sometimes see our predicament if we have a quiet vacation and then step back into the storm at work. We now notice that the pace is frantic and the noise louder.

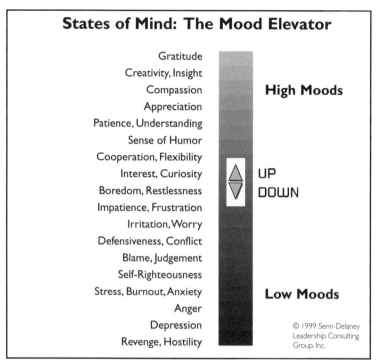

Figure 9.1

Anytime we are at the lower levels of the mood elevator, we don't function well at openness, teamwork, accountability, coaching, change, or any of the other high-performance values or behaviors.

In these lower states we are generally less creative; less able to inspire, motivate, and influence others; and less able to draw the line between our job and our life.

In the higher mood states, we tend to have more perspective. We are not gripped by the discussion, the issue, or the project. A higher state of mind (mood) automatically gives added perspective and allows us to deal with difficult business problems in more creative and effective ways. The higher states enable us to

- Listen more deeply
- Hear the hidden meanings
- Have more wisdom
- Focus on the big picture
- Influence others more

- Worry less
- Keep our bearings despite the turmoil
- Have a better overall quality of life at work and at home

When a team and an organization can learn to operate in a healthier state, they can dramatically increase their performance. They can

- Reach good decisions more easily and more quickly
- Be more supportive internally and more competitive externally
- Align and positively energize the organization
- Handle whatever comes along with greater grace and ease

At Senn-Delaney Leadership we gauge our success as a firm, not only in client satisfaction and goal attainment (revenue, profit, etc.), but also by what we call our Organizational Health.

> ⮑ **Genius/Gratitude**
> ⮑ **Exhilaration/Humor**
> ⮑ **Grace/Ease**
> ⮑ **OK with Stress, Effort, and Crisis**
> ⮑ **Unhappy**
> ⮑ **Troubled**
> ⮑ **Incapacitated**

A few years ago we noted that we were winning in quantitative terms but not feeling good enough about it. We had accepted as normal a state best described as "OK with Stress and Effort." After all, we have big clients with big pressures and big demands. Consulting is not for the faint of heart. It's a tough, competitive world at times. One day during our yearly partner retreat, we looked at each other and said, "It's no fun. Something is wrong."

Today we have a goal to operate our firm more in Ease and

Grace and in even higher states like Exhilaration and Creativity while successfully fulfilling our vision. Despite unprecedented growth and global expansion, we are successfully moving in that direction.

• BE HERE NOW

Have you ever been with a person and he was not there? Have you ever been with a person but you were not there? Have you ever been at home with your family but you were mentally still back at work (and they knew it)? These are all obvious examples of how rarely we are truly present. Here are some less obvious ones.

How many things have you worried about that never happened or were no big deal? Think how much better your quality of life would have been if you hadn't done that.

> **How often do you take a vacation where you really let go of work?**

These are examples of how we miss life and people because we are so rarely present without an overly busy mind.

There is a particular state of mind that almost automatically puts people in a healthier state and a higher mood. It is a combination of a quieter mind and a focus on the moment: We simply call it: *Be Here Now.*

He who lives in the present lives in eternity.

—Ludwig Wittgenstein

It happens every day—two people have a conversation but one or both aren't mentally there. A meeting is held, but the participants never really hear one another. A manager goes home but continues to worry about the office. When people are doing one thing while thinking about something else, they are not really focused on either activity and, consequently, both suffer.

The impact of not being present in the moment is far reaching. An overactive busy mind creates an internal noise level that interferes with creativity and the ability to tap into the reflective, intuitive part of the mind. When our minds are cluttered, we can't really focus on what another person is saying; therefore, we don't really hear them and, therefore, they don't feel heard or respected.

When we can't turn off our whirlpool of thoughts, the quality of both work and home life suffer because we can't give either our full attention. The inability to leave work at work affects our relationships with our loved ones and keeps our batteries from being recharged by a restful, loving home life. This prevents our being fully effective at work.

The ability to focus and concentrate on the moment is what we call Be Here Now. It is a critical skill for maximizing personal effectiveness and fulfillment. With our rapidly changing world and its uncertainty, the importance of balance and focus is more critical than ever.

Gary Mack, a well-known sports consultant and team counselor, teaches professional baseball players to breathe and focus! "A full mind," says Gary, "equals an empty bat!" When a spinning baseball approaches at 95 miles per hour, the batter needs all his focus on the present moment. Any thoughts outside of the present will leave the player standing as the ball goes by.

We all know that peak performance for any athlete, whether a figure skater or a golfer, comes when he is in the zone. He/she is in a flow state without a lot on his mind. That's not just true for athletes. We've all had our moments at work on projects where we seem to be in a flow state, getting a lot done in a less effortful way. This state is active but not stressful, and yet, we are at our best.

Most people also experience times when creative ideas come to them without conscious effort. One large-scale study asked people where they got their best, most creative ideas. The places most mentioned were in the shower, driving to a familiar place that took no thought, and walking in nature. In each of these cases, people had quieter minds, were more reflective, and were more in the present moment.

Some of the many benefits of Being Here Now include:

- Increased productivity and quality when we focus 100% of our efforts on a task and avoid distractions

- Better balance of personal and professional life—if we can be 100 percent present when we're at home and 100 percent present when we're at work, then we will have a rich, nourishing, fulfilling experience in both places

- Easier, more fulfilling relationships—when people feel listened to and appreciated, they more easily develop deep, committed relationships. With a higher level of commitment and sense of self-worth, they produce their best efforts

- Less stress, a quieter mind, and more peace of mind—worries about the past or concerns about the future create stress and reduce our peace of mind. In order to quiet our minds, we need to realize that the past is history and cannot be changed and the future is yet to be and will be determined by the choices and actions of today

Since the health in an organization is a composite of each individual's mood state, here are some hints that can minimize the adverse effects of lower moods and, in time, allow people to spend more time in the higher states, automatically helping the company move to a higher state of organizational health.

1. **Practice Being Here Now at work and at home.** Quiet your mind as you are there for and with others versus being in your own busy thoughts. At work, focus on being present for others to truly hear them beyond the words. Another time to practice it is on weekends. Few people can really leave their work behind on weekends. There are still ways to Be Here Now. If you have blocks of time when you have to work and it really can't be avoided, focus on your work. If you have some hours to play with the kids, be with a loved one or with a friend, BE with them. What doesn't work is to be half there with your work and half present with loved ones.

2. **Be conscious and aware of your mood state.** By being conscious of your current mood, you can be more effective because you can adjust; that is, don't make big decisions in low mood states. Take a break. Go for a walk. Call your best friend and laugh a little. The mood will pass.

3. **When on the lower levels of the mood elevator, remember that thoughts are usually unreliable.** There is a tendency to misinterpret events and actions and see others in a negative light when on these lower levels. A good night's sleep or added perspective will probably make things look different. By just recognizing that you are in a lower mood state gives the mood less power. If you can recognize that this is just a temporary flurry of negative thoughts and not a permanent condition, the thoughts have less power over you. When in the lower states, remind yourself to hold your thoughts lightly; don't grip them for dear life!

A useful metaphor is a horror movie. While watching an engaging, scary film, we can experience some fear. At the same time, at some level we know we are in a movie theater and it's only an illusion.

Our momentary thoughts in lower states of mind about our job, our future, or other people, are rarely what they appear to be, much like the film.

4. **Be aware that in the lower states you are not as effective.** You don't do as well at such things as collaboration, decision making, and problem solving. Just being conscious of your state of mind can be useful. As a general rule, it is rarely a good idea to make a big decision in a lower mood state. Your judgment is impaired and your lenses to the world are clouded.

When you are feeling angry or judgmental, you can't do a good job at giving another person coaching and feedback. Have you ever tried to give a loved one feedback when you (or they) were in a low state? If you had any success, you're very unusual.

Have you tried to collaborate on a team with someone when you both were resentful, untrusting, or judgmental? Once again, it's a design for failure.

On the other hand, teaming, coaching, and creative decision

making all come more easily and naturally in the higher states of mind.

5. **Keep things in perspective.** When you are in a bad mood or in a low state, things that bother you can be all-consuming. You can become gripped by them. Generally, if you look at the bigger picture in your total life, including your health, your loved ones, your other accomplishments, or your life beyond work, things can be put into better perspective.

There are two kinds of perspective that can be of particular help. The first is a "gratitude perspective." In short, this means to count your blessings. Many high-achieving people focus almost solely on what isn't; that includes the goal they haven't reached or what they or someone else hasn't done perfectly. If you merely look at what you have (health, job, loved ones) your spirits are lifted and you are more effective in your jobs and your life.

I carry a picture of my wife and six-year-old daughter and another of a vacation home on the beach in Hawaii. When I'm feeling a little low and it's late at night on the road, or when I'm facing a particularly challenging situation, I take out the pictures to remind myself of my total life and what's really important. That tends to bring perspective.

The second form of perspective is a "humor perspective." An expert on the benefits of humor in the workplace, C. W. Metcalf, says, "Take yourself lightly and your job or problem seriously." Humor automatically puts us in the higher mood states.

The higher mood states are lighter, more creative ones. If someone does something you believe is strange, you have a choice. You can go to the lower states and be "irritated or angry" or you can go to the higher states and be "interested or amused." The latter will give you a clearer head and better mental traction to deal with the situation.

6. **Use Your Feelings as Your Guide.** Sometimes when you are in a lower state of mind, your own "horror movies" seem totally real. The boss is a jerk, your teammate did cross you, your mate isn't understanding, and the world or job is bleak. This inability to have perspective causes you to act when you shouldn't and say things you later regret.

There is an early warning system built into everyone. There is a way to know when our thinking is reliable and when we are wearing dark glasses. It is our feelings. Clear signals of less reliable lower state thinking include:

- Reaction
- Negative intensity
- Anger
- Judgments and resentment
- Despair and hopelessness

Since we each have our own signals, learning to notice the feeling, moderate our behaviors, and discount our lower-states thinking creates a more effective leader and a better overall quality of life.

Higher mood state indicators also exist. They include positive feelings like

- Hopefulness
- Optimism
- Gratitude
- A sense of well being
- Confidence that things can be handled and will work out
- In-the-moment perspective, such as, "My life is more than my job"

These feelings accompany our wisest thinking and a more resourceful, creative, and balanced approach to work and life.

7. **Utilize the thoughts expressed earlier in the serenity prayer.** The less energy you waste in worrying about what you cannot change or in being resentful of "what is," the better your state of mind will be. Remember, more than 90% of what you worry about never happens and, if something is a given, why waste energy complaining or wishing it was different?

8. **Assume innocence in others' actions:** What is the one thing above all else that moves most people down the mood elevator? The behaviors of other people. "They" cause us to be irritated,

angry, impatient, frustrated, judgmental, defensive, etc. While you don't usually realize it or understand it, the intensity of your feelings is directly related to the motives you ascribe to the actions of others. A simple story may best illustrate that.

Let's say I am at the check out counter in a store. I'm standing in line minding my own business and in a pretty good mood when, suddenly, someone rams into me from behind with their cart, and it feels pretty intentional to me. How do I feel? Possibly irritated or maybe angry, upset.

Now I turn around to let this person know what I think and they have dark glasses and a white cane. How might I feel now? Probably understanding, remorseful, a bit ashamed, empathetic.

As soon as I'm about to excuse the action, a guy peeks out from behind the blind man and says, "He's not really blind, he just acts blind so that he can go around ramming people with his cart to get some laughs." How do I feel now? Maybe back to angry and upset.

Just before I let the perpetrator have it, the store clerk tells me not to listen to that guy because he is a pathological liar and tells lies to start fights. The man behind me is really blind. Now how do I feel? I probably don't know anymore. I am confused.

The relationship between my assumed motives and my responses are shown in Figure 9.2. It can run the gamut from being amused to wanting revenge for the same incident:

Assumed Motives

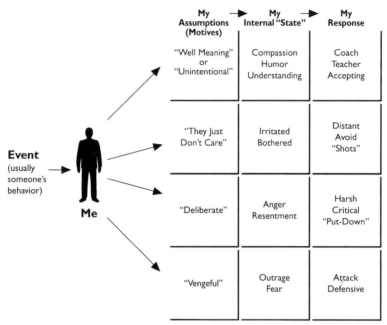

My Assumptions (Motives) →	My Internal "State" →	My Response
"Well Meaning" or "Unintentional"	Compassion Humor Understanding	Coach Teacher Accepting
"They Just Don't Care"	Irritated Bothered	Distant Avoid "Shots"
"Deliberate"	Anger Resentment	Harsh Critical "Put-Down"
"Vengeful"	Outrage Fear	Attack Defensive

Figure 9.2

The notion of seeing innocence doesn't mean that others don't do inappropriate things or things that negatively affect you. It also doesn't mean you don't take appropriate action. The idea of seeing someone's "psychological innocence" merely means you have an understanding that people are always doing what appears to make sense to them based on their thoughts, beliefs, and habits.

By seeing psychological innocence, you are less gripped or bothered by the actions of others. This gives you a healthier state of mind and allows you to deal effectively with the situation.

All too often, teams assume motives in one another or other groups. This leads to more turf-building and lower trust levels. A part of a healthy culture is less focus on other possible motives and just dealing with the facts of the situation. Without a mind full of assumption, the facts and the appropriate response become clear.

A Balanced High-Performance Culture

As a result of our learning as an organization, we now realize that a more complete pyramid of organizational effectiveness would include a healthy state of mind (Figure 9.3). Attention should be paid not only to the values and vision, but also to the state of mind of individuals and the organization. This includes the notion of Higher Mood States, Be Here Now, Seeing Innocence, and being Positive and Optimistic.

Rather than just being another value or organizational principle, states of mind are the determinants of the value system of the organization. An unhealthy (low mood state) organization is predictably dysfunctional in its culture.

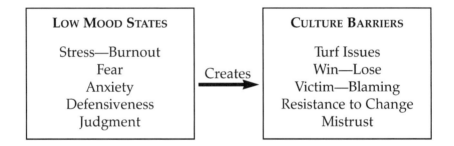

LOW MOOD STATES		CULTURE BARRIERS
Stress—Burnout		Turf Issues
Fear	Creates	Win—Lose
Anxiety	→	Victim—Blaming
Defensiveness		Resistance to Change
Judgment		Mistrust

On the other hand, a healthier state of mind automatically creates the values and behaviors that characterize a healthy culture.

HEALTHY STATE OF MIND/ HIGHER MOOD STATE	A HEALTHY CULTURE
Gratitude Appreciation Curiosity Insight—Creativity Optimism—Hopefulness Sense of Humor	Teamwork Openness to Change Personal Accountability Mutual Respect Openness and Trust Caring About Customers Innovation

Creates →

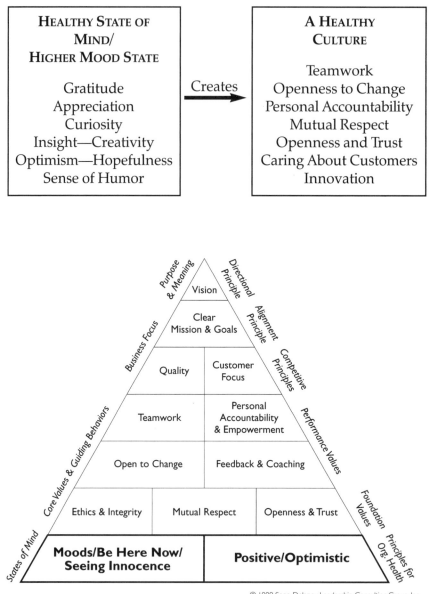

© 1999 Senn-Delaney Leadership Consulting Group, Inc.

Figure 9.3

The High-Performance Culture pyramid provides a visual representation of the building blocks of an effective corporate culture that creates value for customers and consistently moves toward the vision that ignites the organization.

A Process to Discover and Develop Your Own High-Performance Culture

Over the past decades, we have developed several processes that work well in assisting an organization to identify its specific vision and high-performance values or winning behaviors. These proven processes are based on our discovery that vision and values need to come from the heart and not the head. One of the most common errors in defining shared values is that it often degenerates into a highly intellectual and impersonal exercise or series of discussions. Values must come from the heart and soul, not just the head or a flip chart.

A second error that organizations make in writing statements of values and guiding behaviors is doing it in a paternalistic way. Guiding behaviors should be written so that each and every employee in the organization can own them. Statements like, "We will develop our people" perpetuates dependence and hierarchy. A more appropriate statement is "We are committed to continuous personal and professional growth."

To avoid these errors, we have the senior team go to a relaxing off-site location with few business agendas. There, team-building activities and open-ended dialogue allow them to experience new values and new ways of relating and communicating with each other. By experiencing an open, trusting environment, team interaction, and supportive coaching and feedback, they connect at an emotional, not just intellectual, level to the kind of culture they want for their organization and themselves. They also come to understand the power of their states of mind and moods.

This kind of setting is most conducive to identifying the vision and values that touch and move people. Visions and values cannot be developed through a logical, analytical process alone. When people connect very personally to values, they are also more willing to commit to living them. Each company creates its own unique list. The outcome of our own process of creating vision and values at Senn-Delaney Leadership is shown on the following figure:

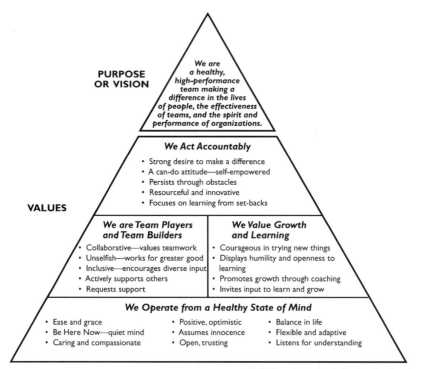

Figure 9.4

10

PHASE V: SUCCESSFUL IMPLEMENTATION OF CULTURE CHANGE

The Power of Beliefs

The culture of an organization is the collective beliefs and habits of its people. Therefore, the real challenge in shaping a new corporate culture lies in shifting the lifelong habits of people. In order to implement a successful culture change, it's useful to understand what cultural habits look like and how they develop in organizations and in people.

Cultural habits are often exposed in the interactive exercises that take place in our Executive Leadership and Culture Change seminars. In one such activity, we put people in pairs and ask them to score points. In most cases they automatically assume that their job is to beat the other person and score more points. If we have multiple pairs in the room, each pair will assume that it has to beat the other pairs. If we divide them into two groups, one group will assume that they have to beat the second group. Beating the other person is not a part of the instructions and not, in fact, how the game is won, yet nearly everyone assumes that's the objective.

What's the root of this strong habit in individuals and in groups? Most of us have grown up taking part in games where there was a winner and a loser. That strong habit, combined with the high internal drive for results of most business executives, leads to the belief that for me to win, someone else has to lose. Over time, this belief becomes an unconscious habit that colors many activities in a person's business life, often at the expense of others within the company. We're convinced that more energy is spent on internal competition in some organizations than meeting competitive threats from the outside.

In the "score points" example we just gave, people see the objective of the exercise through their own filters, including the belief that for them to win, someone has to lose. Since our thought habits largely determine behaviors, and behaviors determine results, the individuals and teams act dysfunctionally.

The influence of beliefs on behaviors and results is illustrated below.

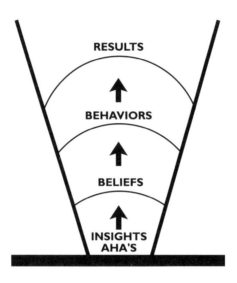

Figure 10.1

A second phenomenon that influences our behaviors can be illustrated by the figure below. What is your immediate impression of what it is?

And what do you see at first glance in the figure below?

If you saw a rabbit in the first figure, you may have missed the duck that is also there. Or vice versa. The same holds true in the figure that has both angels and bats (or devils). The two phenomenon illustrated are Selective Perception and Lock-in/Lock-out. In life we tend to only see a small portion of what is in front of us, only a few of the many personality traits of other people, only one way to view a situation, only one way to look at decisions, and only a few ingredients in culture. The problem is that once we see something in a given way, we tend to lock-in and believe that it is the only way or "the truth."

This all comes together in the "score points" exercise described earlier where people locked-in to a win-lose belief, and then saw everything through that fixed belief. Many of the limiting beliefs we encounter in organizations can be translated into behaviors that are cultural barriers.

LIMITING BELIEFS

Belief		Behavior
It's safest to do what you are told	⇨	Lack of initiative
You can't admit mistakes around here	⇨	Blaming and excuses for lack of results
To do a job well, you have to do it yourself	⇨	Poor delegation
That's not my job	⇨	Narrow focus
The legal department's only job is to avoid any risk	⇨	Stonewalls ideas, no attempt at creative solutions
If I appreciate an employee who's not perfect, they'll slack off and not improve	⇨	No appreciative feedback, lower morale
If I give someone constructive feedback they'll think I don't like them	⇨	Lack of development and coaching
There's more pain for failing than there is reward for succeeding	⇨	Safe, non-risk behaviors
Finance and Controls' job is to police expenses	⇨	Restrictive controls and lack of useful decision tools

---

The kinds of shifts in beliefs that lead to a healthier culture include the following topic areas.

IMPLEMENTING CULTURE CHANGE

In order to change behaviors and reshape a culture, a process is needed to unfreeze these locked-in beliefs and habitual behaviors. The process of unfreezing organizational beliefs is very different from those which are used for the development of organizational structure or a strategic plan. Changing mind-set requires a different learning methodology and process, one that is often less familiar and, therefore, initially somewhat less comfortable for organizations in need of change.

A CULTURE WILL TEND TO REJECT AND RESIST WHAT IT MOST NEEDS TO HELP CHANGE IT

Cultures that are very rational and analytical will only want to use rational and analytical processes to change the culture. Since human behaviors and beliefs are not rational and logical, that's a recipe for failure. In our work with an accounting firm, they wanted to focus almost purely on the Cultural Audit and on measurement. An engineering-based client seemed compelled to diagram the process and analyze it. A banking firm focused on financial rewards. In each case, they tended to avoid and reject the more personal training and coaching needed to shift behaviors. When we did focus on the personal and team behaviors, positive breakthroughs were made.

The successful implementation of a change in corporate culture requires a series of specially designed nontraditional interventions. Research into behavior change has shown that there are two primary ways to modify behavior: One is traditional behavior modification through reinforcement activities such as rewards, punishments, and performance appraisals; while reinforcement is one element of culture change, it is not powerful enough alone to shift an entrenched culture. Behavior modification—including performance appraisal—while necessary, is far too slow in changing behaviors. It is often too indirect and tends to be externally, not internally, driven.

People *do* develop a powerful internal drive to change when they have an emotionally powerful transformational experience. You probably know of at least one business executive who has either had a heart attack or bypass surgery, and the experience was so profound that he wound up changing his ways. The workaholic, cheeseburger-eating person you once knew is now a dedicated runner and somewhat of an evangelist about fat-free foods! Life changed due to a transformational experience. Similar changes are seen following a divorce, the death of a loved one, or the birth of a child. Emotional experience often causes people to step back from their old life patterns, reexamine their beliefs and behaviors, and become committed to rebuilding lives with more balance and meaning than before. The significant emotional event creates an unfreezing and openness for change that didn't exist before, even though the dangers of lack of exercise, poor eating habits, or poor communication at home are all well known.

Similarly, to shift corporate culture, the employees of the organization must have a significant transformational experience that causes them to develop an openness for change that didn't exist before. While this experience can come from such business events as a near bankruptcy, takeover attempt, precipitous drop in sales or income, fear of job loss, or a competitive attack on their core business, these events are external and often create a reactive, fear-driven response. A positive, proactive transformational experience can be created through the implementation of specially designed team-building and culture change seminars for managers and employees. Once employees truly feel the need for change and experience how much better business and personal life can be in a new, high-performance culture, there is a quantum leap in commitment to the change process.

To be most effective in shifting culture, the transformational experience should focus on the values and guiding behaviors that define the desired new culture. By focusing on a new set of business values and daily behaviors that spell out success in the new culture, employees have an opportunity in the seminar to live that new culture, to practice the new behaviors, to discuss the new values and how they apply to work, and to gain a comfort and familiarity with the changes being asked of them.

Since it turns out that the values and the behaviors for corporate excellence are also principles of personal life effectiveness, people end up working to change themselves for themselves, and not just for the company. This makes the change even more appealing and more internally driven. It becomes an inside-out versus an outside-in process.

Once an openness to change has been developed, the old ways of doing things need to be replaced with a set of new business behaviors. If employees gain a readiness for change during the culture-change seminars but come back into the same old work environment with the same old rules, policies, procedures, and supervisory behaviors, it is easy to go back to their old ways and the openness for change is quickly extinguished.

Like the person home from bypass surgery, to effectively change his life, he needs to change his routine. He/she must clean out the refrigerator of unhealthy foods, set up an exercise schedule, and revise his work hours. In a similar way, the company must change daily business behaviors. These most frequently reside in the policies, systems, and procedures that govern the daily activities of employees.

Many of the most powerful policies and procedures lie in the area of Human Resources. For example, to change work behaviors, people need to be evaluated and promoted in accordance with the new cultural values, not the old rules. There are a number of HR systems, including hiring, employee orientation, performance reviews, compensation mechanisms, and others that need to be aligned with the new cultural values.

Another important part of reinforcement is the organization's communications process. An active communications process should be established with newsletters and articles devoted to depicting those employees who are living the new values. In addition, the development of a feedback-rich coaching environment is critical. In such an environment individuals are actively encouraged to coach each other, give both appreciative and constructive feedback, and measure themselves and their teams against the new values and guiding behaviors.

Culture Change =

Transformation + Behavioral Change + Reinforcement
"Unfreezing"   "Shift"

The three high-impact elements in the successful implementation of culture change are:

- Transformational Training—"Unfreezing"
- Revised Human Resource Systems—Behavior "Shift"
- Corporate Communications—Reinforcement

TRANSFORMATIONAL TRAINING

In organizations like GE, training and workout sessions are seen as vital to business success. In all too many organizations, training has often become "nice to do, when we get some extra time or money!" To many senior business executives, training is usually thought of as "motivation," "lecturing," "technical skills development," or "touchy-feely people stuff," and certainly not seen with the same degree of importance as the "hard skills" of strategic planning, product design, financial analysis, or reengineering. While companies will spend millions on strategic planning engagements or reengineering, they balk at spending significant dollars on managerial and employee non-technical training.

In our experience, training is not a "nice to do," but a "must do" for major change initiatives; as well as the only way to successfully shift corporate culture. This is rarely done.

In a *Wall Street Journal* interview, Michael Hammer and James Champy have also come to the conclusion that training is a key ingredient in change initiatives:

> *Hammer: If you're serious about treating people as an asset, we're looking at a dramatic increase in the investment in them. I tell companies they need to quintuple their investment in education....*

Champy: *You also have to teach more behavioral things. Now that we've given you more control, how do you behave and make decisions—from how do you deal with a worker who isn't functioning, to what do you do when a customer asks for something that isn't in the rule book.*

Specialized culture-change trainings are an effective and efficient method of shifting corporate culture. Properly conceived and delivered, these seminars and workshops not only create a shift in the culture, but also prepare an openness for change that allows the reengineering process to take hold and develop.

Traditional lectures or motivational seminars are not effective in shifting corporate culture. While the information may be excellent, culture-shift is not about new ideas or information as much as it is about creating personal change in the employees who comprise the culture. Research has found that individuals best learn that which they experience, as opposed to that which they just hear or read about. In the case of culture change, an old saying aptly applies:

*I hear, I understand; I do, I learn; I **experience**, I **change**!*

The most effective transformational training technology for culture change is what we call "insight-based learning." It produces "ahas" that cause people to reexamine previously held beliefs and habitual behaviors. It does so through structured experiences combined with reflective time that promotes deeper personal and organizational learning.

Training based on the techniques of insight learning can best be described as: a highly interactive process whereby participants take active accountability for their own learning and interact with the material, the facilitators, and the other seminar participants through a series of active discussions, team exercises, personal introspection, group dynamics, business evaluations, and open sharing of ideas and feelings. This more holistic approach allows the seminar participants to integrate the knowledge from the seminar with their own personal experiences. That shifts old habitual ways of thinking and interacting to new, more appropriate and effective ideas and behaviors. It is only through personal change in attitudes and behavior that an old culture can be unfrozen and an openness for culture change developed.

Transformational training is most effective when it is customized and developed for the needs, culture, and style of the organization involved. In most cases, the customization is based on the findings from the initial culture audit, as well as the issues and discussions that surface during the senior management off-site retreat that takes place early in the culture-change process.

To be effective, the culture-change process needs to reach a critical mass of employees before real change can take hold. While culture change must start at the top, just having the senior team experience the change workshop is not sufficient for a real culture shift. One of our early lessons as change-management consultants was that if you want to change your behavior, surround yourself with those who are of like mind and who are willing to coach and remind you. As one of the authors found while training for his first marathon, the support, encouragement, and coaching of a group of friends was essential to develop the new exercise habits it takes to adequately train for a 26.2-mile race!

Our consulting and change management experience tells us that a critical mass of approximately 40–60 percent of employees is necessary before the culture-shift process begins to develop a life and momentum of its own. As more and more people experience the new culture, practice the new skills and behaviors, see the benefits in the new cultural values, and begin to clearly see a new vision of how things could work, the change process begins to gather momentum.

Another highly effective design element in the entire process of culture change involves a cascading approach to the culture change seminars. This starts after the senior session when individual members of the senior team lead their own teams through the culture change seminar. In this way, a participant in the senior session now becomes the leader of their own team session and must become doubly accountable for not only living the new cultural values, but also supporting the overall culture-change process.

We have also found that by conducting the seminars within a natural work group, it is possible to gain peer support and reinforcement and to focus more easily on issues where the newly learned behaviors and change management skills can be used to solve current business problems.

Experience has shown that a broad-based culture-change process is most effective when it is seen as an important company event, and least effective when it is seen as another training program. One has high visibility and relevancy, the other is seen by employees as mere compliance or simply training without any immediate or obvious application to the real world of work.

Revising Human Resource Systems

If you want to get people's attention, fiddle with their pay check.

—Anonymous

As a result of new insights gained during the culture-change seminars, organizations and work teams commit to new behaviors. Reinforcement is vital to maintaining these new behaviors. The most effective reinforcement systems reside in Human Resources. Too often, training programs alone are expected to permanently change behavior. Unless the HR systems, policies, and procedures are altered to be in alignment with the new cultural values, old behaviors will tend to dominate.

For example, to ensure team behaviors, compensation and other reward and recognition systems must shift from the traditional focus on individual performance to a new focus on team and overall company performance. The entire compensation program should be reviewed; including salary, bonus and incentive plans, and job descriptions.

In addition, new hiring profiles should be developed to assist managers in making appropriate selection decisions based on whether people will fit the new culture. Since managers tend to hire in their own image, carefully detailed profiles will enable them to recognize the necessary skills needed in today's business environment and the values and attitudes that match the new culture.

Another key system change that has a great deal of impact on culture and employee behaviors is goal setting, and particularly, the budgeting process. John Davis, CFO for Riggs National Bank of Washington DC, attended a senior management culture-change seminar, along with the other senior officers of Riggs, right in the middle of the annual budget process. Prior to the shared off-site experience, Davis and others were complaining about the difficulty of getting people to cooperate and share resources in arriving at the rolled-up budget figures.

> *Everybody was out to protect their own department and no one was willing to give up resources, people, or most importantly, dollars to support another area of the bank. I've been through dozens of these kinds of 'wars' and it gets really tiring. We finally arrive at a good budget, but the conflict and gamesmanship gets old!*

Following the culture-change seminar, Davis and the senior team finished the budget easily, not because they talked about it during the off-site, but because they all agreed to a new set of team behaviors where the main focus was on what's good for the corporation, not just one individual department. A new set of behaviors—specifically, support and trust—were practiced during the seminar and quickly became the new norm at the top of the organization.

One of the strongest cultural signals is "Who gets promoted and why?" In many ways, the culture is defined and the rules for success are contained in the written, and more importantly, unwritten, promotion policies and examples. In the past, many promotions occurred because of loyalty and tenure. This sends confusing signals about what behaviors are being rewarded, for example, an organization that puts forward the notion that teamwork is an important value and then promotes someone known to be a poor team player.

Additional Reinforcements: Communications and Cultural Symbols

Culture also resides in words, stories, and symbols. Reshaping a culture requires new language, symbols, and words. Since culture change is largely an emotional process, specially developed communications and symbolic reinforcement are needed to reinforce and perpetuate the new culture. Such activities become a tangible vehicle of the transformation and are extremely powerful.

If you want a live example of building the new culture into the work environment, visit the Administration and Corporate Services areas of Bell Atlantic at their offices in Arlington, Virginia. Several floors are plastered with signs, slogans, charts, banners, Blue Chips, and other tangible evidence of The Bell Atlantic Way culture and behaviors. For example, as you walk through the cubicles and down corridors, street signs with such names as "Accountability Avenue" and "Coaching Boulevard" guide employees through their work day. It is easy to feel the energy and spirit of The Bell Atlantic Way behaviors as you enter the floor. At a chance meeting in the men's room on one of the floors, one of the authors decided to test the reality of the culture. Standing next to an employee at the wash basin, he said, "All those signs are pretty neat gimmicks." The person replied, "They aren't just signs; things like accountability are very real around here!"

David Novak set out to create a positive recognition culture at KFC. You can see and feel that by walking down a long corridor called "The Walk of Fame" at their Louisville headquarters. Values are displayed and pictures abound of people being recognized for living those values.

Other appropriate communications include video presentations depicting the values and behaviors of the new culture. Monthly "Dialogue Days" can be set aside for informal meetings on the new values. Newsletters and other publications can feature articles on cultural heroes, and employees should be recognized and rewarded for their efforts wherever possible. Signs and posters can also be used strategically to further communicate the business mission. Navistar has an internal reinforcement audio tape series for their employees that addresses the company's values.

Integration with Initiatives

Creating a healthy culture and winning behaviors can be a part of key organizational initiatives as well as ongoing changes, including:

- Mergers and Acquisitions
- New Leaders and New Teams
- Business Process Improvement
- Total Quality Management
- Restructuring
- Customer Service Initiatives

Teams coming together for any of these reasons can make team agreements that require them to use the healthy behaviors as they work on the initiative. The results can be dramatic. KFC successfully focused their cultural initiatives on creating a new spirit in the stores to increase customer satisfaction and decrease employee turnover. They increased same-store sales and were able to reestablish positive relationships with their 2000-plus franchisees. [*Business Week* on Tricon—October 21-28]

Of equal importance, when the teams succeed, it validates the value of the new culture and ensures its perpetuation.

11

⁂

PHASE VI: MEASUREMENT AND ONGOING IMPROVEMENT

The actions of men are the best interpreters of their thoughts.

—John Locke

What gets measured gets people's attention!

—Anonymous

Like nothing else before, the recent intense focus on workforce improvement and change management is responsible for legitimizing a whole new range of non-financial measurements useful in successfully managing today's complex businesses. Once thought of as soft issues, measures of customer satisfaction, best practices, process cycle time, design cycle time, and corporate culture are becoming important indices. More organizations are developing "Balanced Score Cards" to look at financial performance and beyond. However, it is not easy to measure these less-tangible elements, particularly on the behavioral side.

For years, companies have been attempting to measure the attitude of employees (and by inference, the overall corporation) through the use of morale and opinion surveys. While these have been somewhat useful in recording how people feel about such issues as benefits, supervision, management, service levels, and quality, as a whole they have been ineffective in providing insight into how to improve employee and overall corporate performance. One of the failings of these attitude surveys is that they often depend upon the feeling at the moment, and thus are subject to the normal ups and downs of human personality and quarterly performance.

The results of opinion surveys can change with the announcement of a restructuring or during a difficult labor negotiation.

What is really being measured is how people feel about things, not how individuals and teams are functioning. While feelings are useful in gauging performance, they do not really give us insight into the root causes of performance shortfalls or customer problems.

We believe that attitude surveys are in some way a part of the older business paradigm. They are, in part, a holdover from the unwritten contract that companies had with employees:

We'll take care of you and provide for your security, and you give us your dedication and loyalty.

Since high-performance behaviors and high-performance teams create results for organizations and fulfillment for individuals, it is more important to ask about levels of cross-organizational teamwork than about how people feel. What may seem non-traditional to some is that it is more important to know that there is a bias for action and a can-do attitude than it is to know how unhappy people are about declining medical benefits.

A whole new approach to measuring and monitoring organizational and individual performance is needed to provide today's corporations with a more effective set of performance-improvement tools. Instead of seeking to measure attitudes, we suggest measuring high-performance values and behaviors in actual performance-related activities. When it comes to measuring culture change, what better behaviors or actions to evaluate than the guiding behaviors that constitute the newly desired corporate culture?

In addition, performance measures are more effective and contain more useful information if they come from different sources. Imagine the analogy of a sailor out in the open ocean trying to determine his exact position. Basing current position on the last sighting would be disaster and dead-reckoning would be equally erroneous. Experienced sailors rely on several different inputs or sightings to effectively determine position. Accurately determining corporate culture, individual effectiveness, or other organizational measurements similarly requires multiple inputs.

CULTURAL METRICS: ESTABLISHING BASELINE MEASUREMENTS

The Corporate Culture Profile™, discussed in Chapter 6, is a macro look at the culture taken prior to the culture change. Once the culture has been defined with shared core values and guiding behaviors, it is important to more accurately measure the organization and individuals against those definitions.

An effective individual measure is a 360° Feedback Inventory, which we typically call the Guiding Behaviors Inventory Report™. A similar measurement instrument for the entire organization is called the Organizational Guiding Behaviors Inventory™.

• ORGANIZATIONAL GUIDING BEHAVIORS INVENTORY™

It is relatively easy to build an Organizational Guiding Behaviors Inventory. For each of the shared core values, a list of six to ten specific guiding behaviors can be developed. All employees then fill out an Organizational Guiding Behaviors inventory, rating the degree to which the company is currently displaying these important behaviors during the daily performance of work.

The Organizational Guiding Behaviors Inventory is a snapshot of the culture as it currently exists, measured in terms of the elements in the desired culture. While it is impossible to see culture, or even values, they tend to come to life in these day-to-day actions and behaviors of employees and are effectively measured.

Figure 11.1 shows an example of the summary overview data from a sample Organizational Guiding Behaviors Inventory. The overview lists the composite score for a Core Value category on a scale of one to five. The scores for each Value are the average of all the scores for the six to ten Guiding Behaviors that define that Core Value. As you can see, this organization is currently strong in Leadership, Integrity, and Winning, which indicates a very performance-driven company. At the same time, the company seems weakest in Feedback and Coaching.

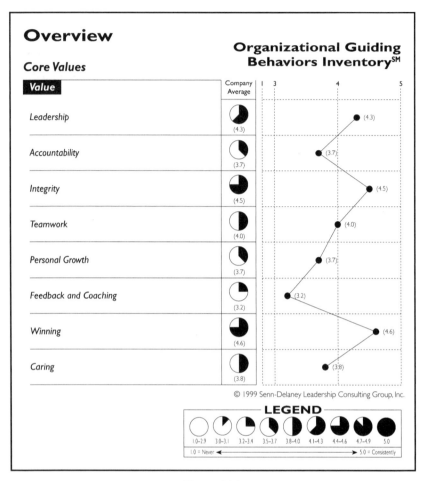

Figure 11.1

Figure 11.1 shows one individual Value, in this case, Teamwork, and the scores for each of the Guiding Behaviors. While the overall average is 4.0, most of the low marks come from people focusing on success for their area or department and not contributing to broader success for the organization. Such daily behavior is particularly damaging when an organization is trying to implement reengineering. As this figure also shows, improvement is needed in the organization on resolving conflict between departments, again indicating that teamwork is strong within, but not across, departments.

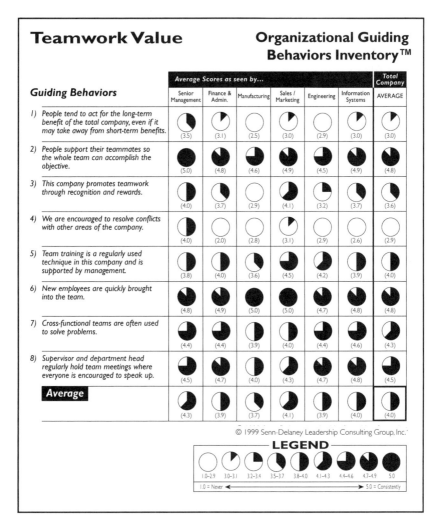

Figure 11.2

It is important to develop an Organizational Guiding Behaviors Inventory™ early on in the process of reengineering and culture change, as this can serve as a baseline measure for the new culture being developed. Once this baseline is established, it will tell the entire organization where they are currently displaying the new cultural values and behaviors, and where the new values and behaviors need greater attention and improvement. By measuring behaviors and activities, not attitudes or feelings, a more accurate representation of the current corporate culture is developed. Using this baseline and performing a simple gap analysis allows everyone to see where the current culture is strong and where it is weak.

Value of Establishing a Baseline Measure of Culture

As with any process of change, and particularly for reengineering and culture change, the Organizational Guiding Behaviors Inventory™ is more than just an event; it's a way of life for that new culture. This cultural "reading" should be taken at least once a year, and during intense times of culture-shaping or change activities, twice a year is appropriate. The value this process provides includes:

- A measurement of the organization's behaviors relative to the Shared Values and Guiding Behaviors

- Feedback on how well the organization is making the new culture a reality in day-to-day activities

- It sends a clear message to the entire organization that living the new culture is important

- It enables the leaders to measure and pay attention to the Guiding Behaviors, which are the greatest levers in sustaining change

- The data can be used to develop action plans for personal and organizational improvement

Once an Organizational Guiding Behaviors Inventory has been completed, we recommend communicating the results to the entire corporation. This will let all employees know how they are living the new culture and what areas need everyone's attention and accountability for improvement. Training programs, discussion groups, and action teams can be formed to focus on those areas of behaviors showing the biggest gaps. With each successive "reading," an organization that is truly committed will steadily grow stronger and stronger as it works to make the new culture a daily way of life.

• GUIDING BEHAVIORS INVENTORY REPORT™

O wad some power the giftie give us to see oursel's as others see us.

—Robert Burns

In these times of rapid change, individuals as well as organizations need to take stock and reinvent themselves. Unfortunately, the majority of managers do not understand their own specific strengths and weaknesses very well. We all tend to see ourselves in favorable light. Recent data shows that only about one third of managers produce self-assessments that match what their co-workers concluded about them.

Even though there is great value in being able see how we come across to others, most people get very little useful feedback on the job. For some, there is no formal feedback; for others, there may be some feedback once a year through the eyes of one person, that is, the boss.

For all these reasons, more and more companies have begun to use a 360° Feedback Inventory that gathers input anonymously from peers, direct reports, direct supervision, and in some cases, the customer or client.

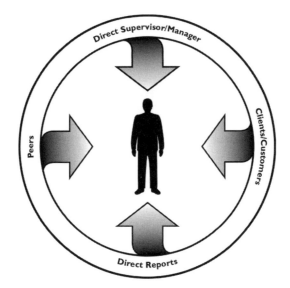

The Guiding Behaviors Inventory Report™ is an exceptional tool for personal development and to see how someone is living the values and guiding behaviors of the new culture. By getting confidential feedback from all directions (peers, direct reports, customers, and immediate manager), an individual can effectively see the shadow they cast in terms of role-modeling the corporate culture. Individuals can instantly create greater awareness of themselves and their impact on others through this process. They will also better understand those areas where they are doing well. A sample profile is shown in Figure 11.3.

Guiding Behaviors Inventory Report™

Personal Profile for John R. Childress

As seen by

Value	All Your Respondents	Self	Manager	Peers	Direct Reports
Leadership	(4.2)	(4.0)	(4.8)	(4.0)	(4.2)
Accountability	(4.3)	(4.3)	(4.4)	(4.1)	(4.3)
Integrity	(4.1)	(4.3)	(4.4)	(4.0)	(4.0)
Teamwork	(3.9)	(4.4)	(4.0)	(3.9)	(3.9)
Personal Growth	(3.8)	(4.5)	(4.0)	(4.0)	(3.8)
Feedback and Coaching	(3.4)	(3.6)	(3.6)	(3.5)	(3.4)
Winning	(4.5)	(4.7)	(4.7)	(4.4)	(4.4)
Caring	(3.6)	(4.3)	(3.9)	(3.7)	(3.6)

LEGEND

1.0–2.9	3.0–3.1	3.2–3.4	3.5–3.7	3.8–4.0	4.1–4.3	4.4–4.6	4.7–4.9	5.0

1.0 = Never ◄─────────────────► 5.0 = Consistently

This chart shows how you are perceived by your respondents, by reporting relationship.

© 1999 Senn-Delaney Leadership Consulting Group, Inc.

Figure 11.3

The Guiding Behaviors Inventory Report™ is a benchmark reading for each individual so that with each successive 360° survey, individuals will be able to see where growth appeared and what areas are still needing improvement. (See Figure 11.4.)

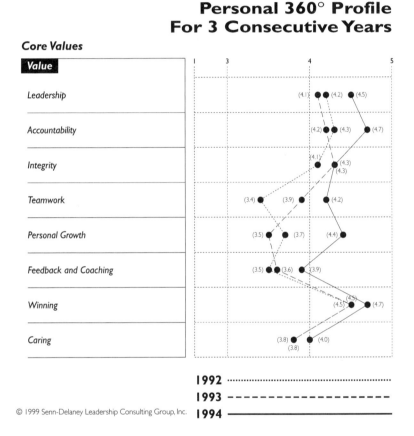

Personal 360° Profile
For 3 Consecutive Years

Figure 11.4

While the 360° Feedback Inventory process has been found to be very valuable, its role is best seen as a supplement rather than a replacement for the employee review process. Anonymous feedback has been found to be more objective when used in a supporting role rather than the primary role in an employee evaluation. The reason is probably because those giving the feedback are more likely to be direct and honest if they know it is not the only input that counts for someone's promotion or lack of it.

A number of leading companies have made significant progress in changing their corporate culture by extending the Guiding Behaviors Inventory Report™ process to the training area as well. For each evaluated characteristic, one or more training programs may be developed that can support an individual to improve their skills and behaviors.

BENEFITS OF GUIDING BEHAVIORS INVENTORY™

- A useful snapshot of how the individual is seen to be living the organization's Shared Values and Guiding Behaviors

- A non-threatening and confidential mechanism for team members and associates to give each other developmental feedback

- A useful road map for improvement

- Increased awareness of leadership abilities and team behavior through precise feedback from the manager, peers, direct reports, and customers

- A vehicle for effective coaching

360° Dos and Don'ts

If we truly want to reengineer a culture, we also need to reengineer the individuals within that culture. Unfortunately, the 360° is usually not developed, utilized, or administered in a way which best promotes the desired culture change. If the 360° is to be a powerful tool in culture change—and it can be—then the following common errors need to be avoided:

- *Don't use a generic or "off-the-shelf" 360°*

The majority of companies use standard or generic 360°s. We believe these are ineffective in shaping a culture. If the culture has been defined in terms of behaviors A, B, and C, and the 360° measures different behaviors D, E, and F, the feedback is not nearly as useful.

For that reason, the 360° should be totally customized based upon the organization's own defined values and guiding behaviors. If teamwork has been defined by five guiding behavior statements, then those same five statements should be used to define teamwork in the 360°. In that way, the 360° can be an exceptional tool to enable the individual to see how he is living the values and guiding behaviors of the new culture.

The initial 360° can become a benchmark for each individual so that with each successive survey, he will be able to see where growth appeared and what areas are still needing improvement.

- **Do start the 360° process with Senior Management**

Based on principles of culture change, the 360° Inventory should be developed and used first by the senior team, including the CEO. It is this group that casts the longest shadow, and if they are not effectively role-modeling the elements and behaviors of the new culture, neither will the organization, no matter how much training or support is given.

When the senior team completes their 360° Feedback Inventory and openly discusses it with their subordinates, much is accomplished. It is a sign of added openness and trust in the culture, and it increases the readiness of the next levels to take part in this process themselves.

- **Don't introduce the 360° in ways that are threatening to people**

All too often, the way in which the 360° is introduced creates anxiety, especially if employees think their jobs may be at stake because of this one measurement. The 360° can be a very positive individual-development tool when administered correctly. People rely on measurement in many day-to-day activities. Look at activities such as dieting, family budgeting, golf scoring, sports ladder standings, health measures, and exercise schedules. We, as critical-thinking human beings, have always rated and will always rate ourselves to see how we are doing from one day to another, in almost any walk of life. Who doesn't have a weight scale in their house?

As long as the results from these measurements are kept private (i.e., how many people know how much you weigh?) and shared at the discretion of the owner of these results, most people view these measures as informative and productive. Once the private results of these measures are made public, the individual is susceptible to comparisons and negative remarks. The measures go from personally motivating to somewhat intimidating.

Likewise, individual 360° scores at work should initially be confidential. As the organization as a whole begins to embrace change and value personal development, more and more individuals will share their performance measures with others in order to benefit from coaching and positive suggestions.

We find that the 360° is readily embraced when utilized in the following format:

- It corresponds with how the culture has been defined according to the values and guiding behaviors of the organization

- It is administered after people have personal exposure to the cultural values in a culture-change seminar

- Confidentiality is ensured by giving the participants a great deal of control over the instrument and by allowing them to hand out the 360° surveys themselves and receive the findings back—without others in the company having access to their results

- The 360° process begins with the senior team and then moves down in the organization

Putting Teeth in Culture Change

If an organization embarks upon a serious culture-change initiative, defines culture, coaches people on behaviors, and then tolerates senior leaders who visibly violate the culture, they jeopardize the entire change initiative.

One CEO, not long ago, told us that several managers had come to him recently to talk about one of their peers, the president of a major division and a direct report to the CEO. They believed the entire culture-change initiative was in jeopardy because, after continual coaching and discussion, this individual continued to behave counter to the newly stated culture and, in fact, belittled the culture-change initiative to employees. Their words to the CEO were, "Many people feel that the culture-change process will lose all credibility if this is the way a member of the senior team is allowed to behave!" Some coaching sessions by the CEO followed and the division president took advantage of an early-out package and retired.

Until recently, most companies would not act on a violation of values other than integrity. A shot was heard around the world by leaders when Jack Welch, General Electric's respected and pragmatic chairman, announced that executives who did not live up to GE's values—even if they produced results—would not have a future in the company. As he told us in our interview:

> *For years we looked the other way while executives drove an organization, intimidated our people, and beat the results out of them to make the numbers. Today, we do not believe this person will make it. We don't believe this behavior is sustainable. We need to live by our values, to energize every mind, and get everybody involved to win in this globally competitive environment. We simply can't have that older leadership style.*

Jack Welch views values as so important that he defines the GE culture through their values and finds ways to ensure that people live the values. Welch has introduced a model describing four types of leaders and how they are evaluated. It is designed to emphasize expected cultural behaviors. They are:

*The **Type 1 Leader** has the values and meets the numbers. That leader is brilliant. We would like a zillion of these. For them it is onward and upward.*

*The **Type 2 Leader** is also easy—that is the leader who does not meet the commitment and does not share our values. While not as pleasant a call, it is just as easy to evaluate.*

*Then you have the **Type 3 Leader**, who has the values and does not meet the numbers. That person gets a second chance. You have got to keep coaching and hoping. And we have some great success stories about this kind of leader changing, although nowhere near the amount we would like. It is well known that we do give people who live the values a second chance.*

*The **Type 4 Leader** is one who meets the numbers but does not share the values we believe we must have. For years we looked the other way—today we do not believe the person will make it over a sustained period of time.*

Leadership Development Model

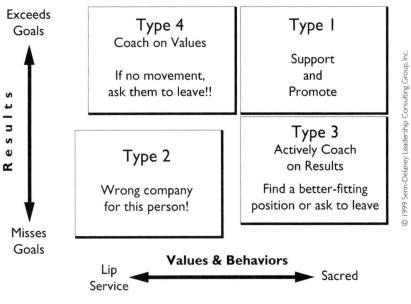

Figure 11.5

Once culture change begins to take on a life of its own, the organization needs to be willing to confront and visibly act on such issues in order to move the culture forward.

OTHER REINFORCEMENT TOOLS

When people are working on changing behaviors to support a new culture, there are a variety of measurement tools that are useful. The most obvious one is the performance management or appraisal system. When explicit values and behaviors are made a part of the review, managers are forced to talk about behaviors with employees. The appraisal system can be made to carry more weight by tying compensation to the guiding behaviors. An energy-services client tied a third of the potential performance bonus to a combination of living the guiding behaviors and efforts to implement the new culture. A large insurance client tied the new cultural values and guiding behaviors to the succession planning process. In fact, the final decision to move the president into the CEO's role was, in part, dependent upon the Board and the retiring CEO's confidence that the new leader would effectively role- model and perpetuate the newly emerging culture, which was seen as a competitive advantage.

Other developmental tools can also be of assistance. In our own firm, we utilize a very simple and useful four-quadrant, behavioral-styles matrix to assist people in learning about their own strengths and weaknesses, as well as helping them understand the importance of diversity and balance-of-life in order to maintain our own healthy culture (Figure 11.5).

Whatever measures or reinforcement tools an organization uses, the key ingredient is the spirit and commitment in which they are utilized by all involved. It takes commitment by the leaders to present these measurements in the best way possible for the organization. Being committed to growing as leaders will only facilitate the openness to growth for the rest of the organization. These measurement tools are the important vehicles to drive culture change through an organization.

12

MAKING A DIFFERENCE

We are in a period of unprecedented change that some liken to the magnitude of the Industrial Revolution. Unfortunately for those doing business today, the same processes no longer apply. Organizations are having to reinvent themselves to be competitive. Business leaders are having to learn new skills to be effective. Employees are beginning to manage their own careers rather than expecting the company to do it for them. This translates into a myriad of simultaneous initiatives including mergers, restructuring, bold competitive strategies, new information systems, customer satisfaction and quality initiatives, reengineering, and EVA.

All of these initiatives are, to a greater or lesser degree, swimming against the tide of organizational habits, which are cultural barriers.

Major transformational changes place a premium on cultural values like

- Cross-organizational collaboration — when turf issues are common
- Empowered employees — when hierarchy prevails
- High levels of personal accountability — when people are feeling victimized, not accountable
- Openness to change — when resistance is prevalent
- Innovation and risk-taking — when a bunker mentality creates risk aversion
- Innovative thinking and wisdom — when people are stressed and frantic

Not only are results diminished by unhealthy cultures, but there is also a human price that is paid as a result of the ineffective implementation of change. This takes the form of:

- Disenfranchised employees
- Loss of loyalty, trust, and commitment
- High levels of stress and burnout
- Poor balance in life and neglected families

The answer to superior competitive performance and more fulfillment for people can be found in the qualities of a healthy culture and an enlightened 21st-century style of leadership.

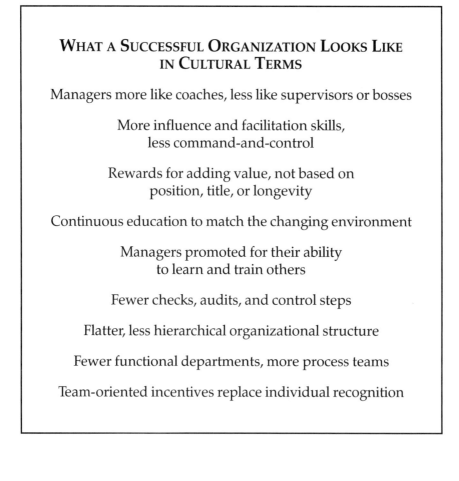

WHAT A SUCCESSFUL ORGANIZATION LOOKS LIKE IN CULTURAL TERMS

Managers more like coaches, less like supervisors or bosses

More influence and facilitation skills,
less command-and-control

Rewards for adding value, not based on
position, title, or longevity

Continuous education to match the changing environment

Managers promoted for their ability
to learn and train others

Fewer checks, audits, and control steps

Flatter, less hierarchical organizational structure

Fewer functional departments, more process teams

Team-oriented incentives replace individual recognition

A Model for 21st-Century Leadership

During times of active change, everyone in the corporation has a leadership role and an obligation to lead!

We urge managers at all levels within organizations not to be bystanders or victims during these times of change. Whether or not an organization is actively addressing its cultural or leadership issues, a difference can be made.

Everyone influences the culture around them; in their organization, their department, or their own work team. Each of us casts a shadow by our own behaviors and each of us has a choice in terms of our own personal and professional development.

In addition, organizational transformation does not take place without personal transformation. If everyone waits for those above them or around them to change, no one changes. This is the time when all individuals need to take a look at themselves and decide ways in which they can change in order to more effectively deal with the changing times.

At the end of the year, many people make a list of New Year's resolutions to be more effective. As we approach the 21st century —a new millennium—it is the time we make our resolutions on how to move toward becoming 21st-century leaders. To facilitate that movement, we have identified a few of the leadership transitions already underway.

TRANSITIONS TOWARD LEADERSHIP
IN 21ST CENTURY

From Earlier Paradigm ⇨	*To Current and Future Paradigm*
Being a manager	Being a leader
Being a boss	Being a coach and facilitator
Controlling people	Empowering people
Holding on to authority	Delegating authority
Micro-managing	Leading with vision and values
Directing with rules and regulations	Guiding with winning shared values
Relying on position power and hierarchy	Building relationship power and networked teams
Demanding compliance	Gaining commitment
Focusing only on tasks	Focusing on quality, service, and the customer
Confronting and combating	Collaborating and unifying
Going it alone	Utilizing the team
Judging others	Respecting, honoring, and leveraging diversity and differences
Changing by necessity and crisis	Committing to continuous learning
Being internally competitive— (win/lose)	Being internally collaborative— (win/win)
Having a narrow focus, "me and my area"	Having a broader focus, "my team, organization"

FINAL THOUGHTS ON CHANGE INITIATIVES

For those organizations and individuals embarking upon major change initiatives, we would make the following recommendations:

- Get as committed to culture change as you are about competitive improvements. Utilize change-management processes and culture-change trainings to simultaneously address leadership skills, teambuilding, and culture change

- Engage in culture change concurrently with business change initiatives to maximize efficiency and provide synergy. They will support one another

- Don't start unless you're serious. Starting and stopping creates incredible frustration and alienation among employees

- Don't quit, even if it looks like things are not working. Usually it's just a need to persevere and make certain you are getting everyone involved in the process

- Counsel your resistors, in or out—especially those among senior management. There is no room for spectators in the process of reengineering and culture change

- Communicate—Appreciate—Communicate

- Celebrate the little wins along the way

- Laugh (a lot): It's therapeutic for everyone!

FINAL THOUGHTS ON CULTURE

All that you do or attempt to do in your organization will be influenced by your culture. Therefore, you might want to keep the following in mind:

- Your organization has a culture whether you want it to or not

- The only choice you have is whether you proactively influence the culture or not

- Whether you lead a company, a department, or a team, you influence the culture of that group by the shadow you cast. Who you are and how you behave speaks louder than any words you use

- A healthy, high-performance culture is the greatest asset an organization or team can have

- Even though these are turbulent times, you can operate without undue stress if your organization has a healthy culture and you maintain a healthy state of mind

- Cultures can be systematically shaped. It just takes a different technology and a commitment to do it

ABOUT SENN-DELANEY LEADERSHIP

The Senn-Delaney Leadership Consulting Group was founded in 1978 with a specific mission: Assist CEOs and senior executives to create High-performance Teams and Winning Cultures. Today, Senn-Delaney Leadership is a global firm known for its experience and accomplishments in the areas of Culture-Shaping, Teambuilding and Leadership Development. While management consultants work on formulating strategy, structure, systems, and processes, we as leadership consultants focus on creating the organizational and team effectiveness needed to ensure those change initiatives work.

High-performance teams and winning cultures are of utmost importance today. Research and experience confirm that the shortfall in most change initiatives is due to the human issues, not the technical ones. This is true for mergers, new leaders, new strategies, restructures, IT installations, and all other major changes.

For over 20 years, we've worked with corporate leaders in the Energy, Information Technology, Financial Services, and Consumer Products/Diversified industries. Our clients include: Agilent, Toys "R" Us, Bell Atlantic, Pacific Bell, Sprint, British Telecom, British Gas, Commonwealth Edison, Portland General Electric, Florida Power and Light, Compaq Computer, IBM PC Division, Hewlett Packard, McDonald's U.S., PepsiCo, Bank One, GTE Information Services, and Rockwell International. We have also aided the merger and acquisition transition process within organizational recombinations such as: Chemical-Chase Bank, OhioEdison-Centerion, Southwestern Bell-Pacific Bell Directory, Compaq-Digital, and Bank One, First Chicago, and National Bank of Detroit.

As we approach and enter the new millennium, the professionals of the Senn-Delaney Leadership Consulting Group remain committed to our vision of "Making a Difference Through Leadership™."

For additional information about the consulting services
of Senn-Delaney Leadership, please visit our website at:

www.senndelaney.com

Senn-Delaney Leadership
Part of the Provant Solution

3780 Kilroy Airport Way
Long Beach, CA 90806
Phone (562) 426-5400
Fax (562) 426-5174

INDEX

T

Tylenol tampering incident, 58

V
values
core values, 93, 95
defining guiding behaviors, 109–110, 137
defining values, 137–138
definition, 57
foundation values, 95–105
GE's Leaders' Values, 19, 21–22, 21–22
in high-performance cultures, 93–109
The HP Way, 19–20, 55
importance of, 91–92
internalization of, 65
leadership and. *See* leadership
measurement of living the values, 155–156, 160–161
performance values, 100–109
shared values and beliefs, 20–21, 57–60
winning values, 93
See also beliefs
victim attitude, 102–103, 105, 135
Virgin Group, 86
vision, 29, 38, 39, 68, 110–115
"Vital Few" (developed by Houghton), 88

W
Wal-Mart, 28, 60, 85
Walton, Sam, 60, 85
Waterman, Robert H., 20
weak cultures, 48–49
Welch, Jack, 21
on change, 14, 33–34, 107
on culture, 92
leadership development model, 165–167
on values, 59, 95
See also General Electric
Westinghouse Electric Corporation, 12
The Wisdom of Teams (Katzenbach and Smith), 102
Wittgenstein, Ludwig, 127